A PROCESS for

Developing a New Approach to Living

Bruce Robert Hanson

After 40 years of self-discovery

A Process, for Developing a New Approach to Living

v1.0

ISBN: 978-0-9993238-0-9

Cover Art by Mallory Rock

E-book formatting by Mallory Rock and Melissa Stevens

PRINTED IN THE UNITED STATES OF AMERICA

DEDICATION

Dedication of these thoughts is made to the person most instrumental
to the transformation I have experienced in my life,
my ex-wife Janet Teresa (Donovan) Hanson.
She was a charming, creative, beautiful and sensitive and emotionally fragile person
who struggled and ultimately lost the battle with her demons through the abuse of alcohol to numb her pain.

During our life together, I raged at the chaos in our lives and I did so with self-righteous arrogance.
I withheld my love and affection as a punitive act to show my contempt.
I demeaned her weakness, only making her low self-esteem worse.
I divorced her out of justified anger and felt power in my resentment.

Were it not for the utter shambles my life had become, I would not have sought change.
I had nothing after the divorce; my house of cards completely fell apart.
I was literally homeless, directionless, broken and desperate.
Consequently, I was able to start with a clean slate without demands or preconceptions.

I was fortuitously led to a community of people who loved me
before I could love myself.
They listened to my vulgar rantings without judgment and spoke about
a strength they had used to overcome situations that, in some cases, were worse than my own.
I slowly began rebuilding from the inside out and found a place in connection with others I had not known or thought was possible.

Gratitude does not begin to express the appreciation I feel for having been brought to my knees.
It started with the combustion between opposing self-wills.
And the journey of self-discovery will continue daily through my quest to maintain inner peace.

Janet is gone now. I can never express directly to her my humble appreciation
for her forcing me to face myself. Dedicating these writings to her is, in small measure,
my way of expressing my most heartfelt thanks. This is the thanks I have for
catastrophic-creative-transformation I found in my process.

FOREWORD – WRITTEN BY DENNIS KIRKMAN, PH.D.

I've never met a compulsion I didn't like. Well, with the exception of gambling and smoking. These days, I can't get enough of crossword puzzles and my latest, Sudoku. I am the classic first-born child—overachiever, people pleaser, high need to control. I've had a modicum of success, but those traits that helped me succeed can lead to my undoing from time to time, and have. I grew up in a working poor family. Young uneducated parents, first generation to the city from the farm, they could barely manage their own lives, much less their children's. Dad struggled with a head injury from his youth with poor impulse control and executive function, and Mom was orphaned and passed around as a child—after her father had been murdered. The main methods of interacting were physical and shaming, both handed out vigorously. The role that was most acceptable for me was the family clown. If I could make them laugh, they'd be OK with me. Any other kind of expression was not allowed. We didn't have conversations. To this day, I find it often difficult to be conversational for fear of being judged. It is easier to hide behind my "role" and intellect, which, I know, further distances people.

Time and again throughout my life, the core feeling of shame and unworthiness would trump my best efforts at controlling outcomes that I thought would make me happy, resulting in the chaos I sought to avoid.

I had been in therapy for years both as a person needing help and my own training as a psychotherapist. I would eventually leave that world some 30 years ago to start my own business. A different clinical aspect, but more managing a group than the intensely interpersonal therapy session.

I first saw Bruce at a group support meeting after a devastating family event occurred in my life. I thought I understood people, but I knew nothing about the addictive process that had occurred. Over the years, I came to admire Bruce's honesty, commitment to the truth, and his compassion. And, when the issue of addiction raised its head again, I sought Bruce out.

I have learned many things over the years during our regular coffees together. Simple principles, yet doggedly difficult to integrate: concepts of willfulness to let go of being right, the feelings of power from controlling for outcomes. With his help, my despair and confusion would gradually turn into a flourishing acceptance as I became comfortable in my own skin.

Bruce would be the first to admit that it was not necessarily his personal skills or aura that accomplished for me, and for many others, what is possible. Rather, it was his steadfast living of the principles he talks about here in this book, translating that through the caring and compassionate person that he is.

There is no question that we live in a world where the onslaught of information and choices for stimulation are beyond our brain's ability to synthesize. It's not a surprise that a very large issue we are facing as a society is the rising costs of addictions and compulsive behaviors. Our brain is hardwired for pleasure; dopamine is a powerful motivator and there is no shortage of opportunities to press that lever again and again, just like the rats did in my old psych labs. Many of us, some highly functional, some struggling, experience the same diminution of life experience in our pursuit of and obsession with escape.

Bottom line is, we want to be happy and I would argue that we deserve that, but as Bruce would say, it's an inside job, and he does well here in providing some practical tools. Through case stories he illustrates key points of a change process, and offers exercises that are highly illustrative and enlightening for those who would be teachers as well as for their clients. By Bruce's prolific and large commitment to service and giving back I would estimate that he has helped many dozens of people lead healthier, more productive lives. He has truly made a difference in his community, and his book reflects that ongoing giving back of the lessons he has learned and those of others.

In the book, Bruce takes readers on a step-by-step journey of how he applies principles generally applicable to everyone experiencing serious problems in living. His consistent rejoinder to me over the years of just two of the many truths—letting go of a problem and allowing the universe/a higher power handle it; and, when we are in conflict, remembering that everyone is really doing the best they know how—has helped me tremendously with a divorce crisis, the changing relationships of my adult children, and transitions in my business.

Bruce talks frequently about courage and change, and the courage to change. Most research indicates that when people try to change a core issue, they generally need to make multiple attempts. That's the reason Bruce emphasizes that point and makes the case that this kind of change is more likely in the context of the Other: another person, a group, a higher power. It's through the act of transparency that the real self can emerge in an accepting environment. Because finally being authentic is so intrinsically rewarding, personal growth can get a foothold and supplant compulsive and isolating behaviors.

I agree with Bruce when he says that the principles he describes are universal and have been taught for a very long time. These are practical methods derived from our oldest spiritual traditions, and independent of theology, they are practical applications of psychological hygiene in everyday life. (Additionally, the process that Bruce describes puts those applications in a psychodynamic and cognitive context—that our past and, in particular, family of origin issues, continue to affect how we perceive ourselves and the world, leading to faulty ways of thinking.)

As I've said, the apparent simplicity of the concepts is misleading. They can be difficult to take seriously or put into practice, but if they are, they are very powerful. For example, *"practicing an attitude of gratitude"* even in my darkest hours has helped me reframe situations and persevere. Gratitude found a place in my business also. About 15 years ago I instituted a monthly special meeting of all staff at my company. All employees gathered around a large table and we would talk about the good things that we were doing, client success stories, and recognizing others' contributions. It is the most morale-boosting activity that I have ever used or been a part of. We still have that meeting and I am always thrilled to be there and, especially, to see how new employees respond. Group gratitude is powerful.

We all want to be loved, I believe. Somebody once said in one of those meetings that the brain doesn't recognize the difference between receiving and actively giving love. And when I heard that I thought it adds a whole new layer of meaning to the exhortation to "Love thy neighbor as thyself." I tried it and I found it to be true. The statement changed in my mind from the scriptural command I always heard as a child to sound practical advice on how to live a happier life.

By keeping an open mind, I believe that the book offers practical solutions to helping people become more authentic, and more satisfied with their relationships and life. Bruce would say, though, *"Keep what you need and leave the rest."*

PURPOSE

All of us have struggles that lead to a less than desirable quality of life due to a deep-seated feeling that something is wrong and can't seem to be fixed. Because of the persistence of these struggles, a nagging sense of being defective, incapable, even unworthy begins to define us as something we don't like and never intended to be. Over time, this condition develops into an internal reality expressed with resentment, negativity and withdrawal. We seem trapped and either fight against such unseen forces or resign ourselves to our helplessness.

This book serves as a framework for those looking to resolve this internal conflict. It is to be used both as a self-help book and as a tool for those in a position to impact someone else's life. Such people may be teachers, human resource managers, members of the clergy, or other mentors, those in positions to be "coaches" where they can help others, "their clients," apply the principles suggested in this book. This stated purpose is not meant to exclude mental health professionals, but the approach outlined here is not purposely patterned after any of the traditional clinical modalities and does not claim to be an alternative to the valuable process of mental health counseling.

The term coach is used throughout the book as a generic term where it is expected that the coach will use this book, as well as other materials, to provide guidance to clients in their personal development. Ideally, both coaches and clients will use the book as a tool to help achieve positive personal growth. The clients will read the material for each stage, complete the corresponding exercises, and review completed work with their coach.

Although the information included in this book can enhance the lives of men and women alike, it is written from a male perspective. Because the manuscript is based on my personal knowledge and experience with the subject matter, I felt it only fair to write from the gender perspective I know best, that being male. As a result, I occasionally refer to an individual as "he." My work during the past twenty years has focused on men and their healing, and it was through these experiences that I created the following book. I wanted to create a book that is based on what I know to be true, and yet has the capacity to heal anyone willing to undertake such a feat. That being said, the process outlined in this book is incredibly powerful and has the capacity to change lives, regardless of gender, age, or life circumstance.

It is important to note that the approach I have outlined here is neither original nor particularly innovative in its illumination of certain principles. It is based on a general concept that has been practiced in different forms, with different terminologies and using different rituals throughout history, and is an approach that appears time and again in both ancient and contemporary literature. In essence, this approach forms the basis for many widespread movements in history, many of which have promoted positive personal growth.

This book is a modest version of principles that promote positive change. I have included in the book numerous unreferenced, italicized passages that have been passed along by those individuals willing to share their wisdom, the wisdom they achieved through hard-fought experience. It also serves as a testament to the existence of a "*life force*" that reminds us all that insight into life's lessons is abundantly available, and yet only a few are able to hear its melody, feel its rhythm, or find the wavelength of its harmonics.

Many people will view the process in philosophical terms; others view it as religious, or still others as psychological. The truth is that all schools of thought add to the lexicon of inner personal work. Each school of thought is important and any combination of two or all three provides additional dimension. This attempt to codify a process is designed to use words other than those that are familiar, as well as offer a fresh perspective to these age-old principles.

A process works through simple concepts: honesty, integrity and humility. Without a willingness to be completely honest, this process does not and likely will not work. As humans, we resist uncertainty; this is simply human nature. We abhor being confused because of the fear of appearing ignorant or feeling lost. It is natural for us as humans to hold on to preconceived notions and avoid the unknown. We create plausible narratives about how things work in order to feel a sense of security and continuity. These narratives appear to explain ourselves and our place in the world. But, without a willingness to delve deep and explore, we lose sight of our inner context, failing to recognize the internal broiling conflict. Complete honesty is vital to get to the core of one's nature—of our human nature.

How does one define honesty? Honesty, in this case, is coming to recognize our individuality, our unique reality; it entails understanding the distinction between ourselves and others, embracing our true nature and living comfortably in concert with the forces we cannot see, understand, or ultimately control. Honesty pairs with integrity and humility in this process. Integrity requires a genuine commitment to our truth without the need for recognition or approval. Humility, then, freely gives others the right to their own truth, permitting them to own and live their integrity.

This outline is presented logically and linearly, like a formula that guarantees positive outcomes. However, this is not the case. While there is an intellectual component, the process is designed for those who are compelled, not by logic, but by the burning need to seek inner peace. Individuals who know this pressure know that it builds over years of a growing dissatisfaction. Oftentimes these same individuals refuse to wait any longer for relief, and they are the ones willing to adopt an approach like the one I am proposing. They are also the candidates who demonstrate unyielding motivation, who will stop at nothing to make complete and lasting change.

I encourage you to read the book, gleaning from my insights the ways in which this process can transform your life. Enjoy.

INTRODUCTION

It's all about CHANGE.

While this book is about inner personal change, let's first step back and look at a broad perspective of the idea of change. Change is both complex and difficult as seen historically at the macro as well as the micro level. Without meaning to be too academic, I ask you to recognize that change has been studied and experienced through the ages and continues to stir discussion and controversy. In other words, change is not to be taken lightly because its effects can be dramatic and profound.

The word "change" has shifted in meaning over time. In previous times, the word mainly referred to changes in the external world: objects, governments, organizations, conditions. Many of the ideas of external change have their foundations in economic thought. While the recorded history of economics dates all the way back to the ancient Greeks, more modern economic philosophers include Adam Smith[1] and John M. Keynes.[2] These great thinkers applied logic to their theories. They also used the approach of a growing scientific method in the nineteenth and

1   Adam Smith (16 June 1723 – 17 July 1790) was a Scottish Ethics pioneer of Political Economy. He is best known for two classic works: The Theory of Moral Sentiments, 1759 and The Wealth of Nations, 1776
2   John M Keynes (5 June 1883 – 21 April 1946) was a British economist. His ideas fundamentally changed the theory and practice of Macroeconomics and the economic policies of governments.

twentieth centuries to develop a perspective that change is both understandable and predictable.

More recently the idea of inner personal change has become a popular topic. Our current perspectives on inner personal change come from the psychological pioneers Sigmund Freud[3] or Carl Jung.[4] This is reflected in the modern-day expansion of the treatment industry with its growing army of therapists, innumerable psychopharmacological drugs, and array of inpatient and outpatient treatment facilities. The increasing awareness of personal dissatisfaction has also, unfortunately, resulted in a burgeoning number of people suffering from prescription and nonprescription medication addictions. This is an unfortunate and dire consequence of people seeking an escape from inner turmoil.

Mental health treatment is an extremely valuable tool in the modern arsenal of quality of life enhancements, yet some are skeptical to become involved in that method to achieve change. They remain hesitant to seek mental health counseling because doing so sounds daunting: the length of the time commitment required (perhaps years), the lack of insurance coverage, not to mention potential confusion surrounding how talk-therapy brings about enlightenment.

It is also human nature to dislike change. We need only look to history for proof. For example, what happened to the most

---

3   Sigmund Freud; (6 May 1856 – 23 September 1939) An Austrian Neurologist and the founder of Psychoanalysis.
4   Carl Gustav Jung; 26 July 1875 – 6 June 1961) A Swiss Psychiatrist and Psychoanalyst who founded Analytical Psychology.

famous leaders? What happened to those who have posed controversial questions?

"Where are our leaders? Where is Socrates, the Christ, Abraham Lincoln, Gandhi, Martin Luther King, Malcolm X? They were all murdered."

Why? Because these courageous men brought forth radical ideas that challenged the established social order. And those in power rose up and refused to allow change to take place. Instead, they took their own radical measures in order to maintain the status quo.

Resistance to change happens at the personal level as well. Preconceived notions, prejudices, biases, or beliefs are foundational to life itself; we defend these beliefs with fierce determination and this is reflected in our behavior, attitudes, and actions. The prospect of undertaking a process to reconstruct our life patterns and the way we experience life is, for the most part, considered heretical. Consider the difficulty many Catholic couples have with the idea of divorce because of church teachings that are considered inviolate. It is so much easier to hold on to our taboos rather than to expend the emotional energy to question, let alone change, what is believed to be true.

The process I am suggesting in this book acknowledges that personal change requires courage and commitment at a level a person has not likely experienced before. When reading this book and approaching the process, I urge you to remember that *courage is not the absence of fear, but rather the recognition that there is a purpose in one's pursuit that has greater value than the fear being experienced.* Engaging in any personal growth process requires true courage and yet, it is one of the supreme experiences of humanity since the dawn of time.

<u>Organization of A Process</u>

This approach is made-up of Twelve Stages, divided into three main topics.

The first main topic is **Insight**. The emphasis in this section is coming to terms with how you currently live your life, specifically your habits, behaviors and attitudes.

> Stage 1 - Look inward and revisit the context of your family of origin.
> Stage 2 - Recognize the core beliefs or worldview you adopted during early development.

From these exercises, patterns and insights will emerge.

> Stage 3 - This strengthens your commitment to change.

The second main topic is **Discovery,** which refers to the impact that habits, behaviors, and attitudes have had on your life. This section is made up of six separate stages:

> Stage 4 - An exhaustive accounting of your character traits.

Stage 5 - Become transparent about these traits.

Stage 6 - Put the traits into quantitative terms.

Stage 7 - Adopt humility so that changing these traits can take place.

Stage 8 - Acknowledge the impact that these traits have had on others.

Stage 9 - Define the changes you intend to make.

The final main topic is **Implementation** and is covered by the last three stages:

Stage 10 - Commit to and practice ongoing accountability.

Stage 11 - Experience a balanced and meaningful existence.

Stage 12 - Live your life in service to others.

Within each Stage, I illustrate an application of the concepts through a story. These stories are patterned after real people but may involve a composite of two or three individuals. Therefore, the names used are fictitious and the details of place and circumstances have been modified to ensure the privacy of those mentioned. While these individuals have done a good deal more work than is suggested in the stories, these episodes characterize key principles used to make progress. It is not necessarily important that you relate directly to each story; however, it is important that you (and your client) understand that the process works, and that it is available to anyone who will *thoroughly follow a programmatic approach*.

How to Get the Most Out of This Approach

Change is more likely to occur in a person's life when three supporting elements are pursued simultaneously. These include:

1. undertaking a programmatic method,
2. pursuing the approach with a belief that it WILL work and
3. surrounding oneself with others who also believe in the efficacy of the approach and who have gained benefit from applying it in their lives.

The critical nature of a programmatic method (like what I will be mentioning in this book) is that there is a beginning that leads incrementally to improving existence. Consequently, the first exercise must be completed before moving on to the next, because there is a cumulative effect as each new stage is started and completed. More importantly, true transformative change does not take place until all phases are thoroughly completed, in order, and with dedication. It is vital to understand that the purpose of this undertaking is to achieve dramatic and powerful change; thus, no one should ever pretend to be a student of this, or any process, unless he is fully dedicated to it, even when it proves difficult.

Belief is an equally important element for lasting success in this program. For example, a person would probably not start on a journey to a foreign location without the belief that he had the means and commitment to arrive at the destination.

People might not know all the circumstances they may face along the way: the car may need repairs, there may be detours because of washed-out bridges, they might lose time because of a wrong turn. But, they hold the belief that they are capable of making it to their destination safely. While it is okay to remain aware that unknowns exist, there is never a doubt that they are fully capable of completing the journey. This is belief at its best, when we accept without evidence that we must undertake a journey, even when the opposing arguments sound convincing.

Applying yourself to a process of change is done with commitment and enthusiasm, particularly when it involves fellowship with others. When we are in the company of other like-minded people who share the same values, we are more willing to follow the approach; we have a stronger sense of not only what is being asked, but of its value, its promise. Camaraderie can be a powerful motivator; others can attest to the benefits, they can share stories of how they completed difficult tasks, offer encouragement and remind us of the tremendous positive possibilities. They can make the process seem doable and worthwhile. Such is the nature of community, such is the development of tradition, and such is the codification of belief.

For those considering positive personal growth, I suggest a programmatic approach, like the one contained in the following document. The theory is based on the belief that the process will work for most people who complete all the stages. The process also comes with a community of people who share this path. If you choose to study what is on the following pages, remember, you are not alone. It is vital to understand that any self-examination and any issues you discover in the process are not unique; rather, they are shared by many. They are part of being human. The liberating principle of this work is that *one's character traits make one human; one's honesty about one's character traits makes one lovable.*

If you decide that the next step on your journey is to follow this process, you should first open a calendar to schedule when sessions between you and your coach will occur, and set aside designated times for all reading and writing assignments to be completed, ideally on a weekly basis. Then, set up a computer folder with subfolders for each stage of the process, so you can enter and edit the written assignments. You and your coach will review each assignment during the session. Set a time when assignments will be completed and shared with your coach prior to a formal review meeting. Do not take anything about this process lightly. It is some of the most important work you will do in your entire life.

A PROCESS

PHASE I: INSIGHT

I use the term **INSIGHT** to characterize the first three stages of this process because first, you must step back to see the big picture of your life. Most people possess a belief of who they are, their abilities, their failings, their character, their place, and then they carry this belief deep inside, not as cognitive thought but more like a demonstrated image. This belief permeates every action, choice, attitude, and relationship. Typically, people are unaware of these connections. Instead, they experience discord between the beliefs in their core and react negatively when external circumstances don't match their beliefs.

Our core beliefs often reveal themselves in unique, not so subtle ways. Many people present a public persona that is different from what they feel, in an attempt to alleviate any inner unease they experience. Some use anger to protect themselves. Some approach this disconnect by creating a narrative that aims to reconcile life's great mysteries, all the while never fully addressing their own humanity. Still others experience a sense of brokenness, lapsing into despair and martyrdom, with no clue as to what to do or where to go.

Others act superior, convinced they are gifted and should be granted success and know truth. These types of individuals are insufferable; they suck the oxygen out of their environment and appoint themselves to direct others using dominating personalities, and they do this in every environment.

1

Unfortunately, these types of people lack all of the essential ingredients to pursue inner personal change. Instead, they approach life as being entitled and disdain any thought of being one of the least in society. These people are likely to remain wrapped in the cocoon of their own self-righteous arrogance until they experience a catastrophic event.

These are only a few examples of the places people may find themselves when beginning this process. Because you have likely not faced these traits directly, you must undertake the following exercises with fresh eyes. You must not rely on previously held self-images. This is a deep dive into the past and present and requires three distinct stages.

> **Stage 1:** You can view these issues that have prompted you to begin this process from a structural as well as historical perspective. I use the analogy of structure because adults have built a way of life integrating thoughts, feelings and beliefs into an edifice, clad with behaviors and attitudes. When revising the structure, you study the foundation, the framing and the mechanical systems that lead to some de-construction before the new work can begin. It is equally important to consider history because things change over time. Greater sophistication and maturity have been added to the original supporting members. Until you take the time to dissect the structure, it is impossible to know the true nature or extent of necessary reconstruction.

> **Stage 2:** This work entails sorting out fact from fiction, bringing you face to face with reality. Fact, in

this case, is identifying and reconciling your public persona as the fictional social camouflage it truly is. I illustrate this idea by the statement: *Just once I want to go to the masked ball dressed only as myself so no one will recognize me.* Ignoring or hiding from your true self is exhausting. This exhaustion stems from the incessant attention you must pay to make sure that the "internal" calculations remain consistent, that your true self doesn't accidentally leak through the mask. *Coming out* from behind the facade is necessary for real change. Coming to accept that change is possible once you face your erroneous truth, once you catch a glimpse of life without subterfuge—these are the elements of hope.

Stage 3: Here, I address the idea of embracing what is necessary to achieve a new reality. Knowing what changes need to take place is only an initial step. More importantly, you need to make a commitment to pursue change. This is an act of conviction, a willingness to see that what has been in the past is unacceptable and will dissolve. It is also trusting that what you desire will ultimately bring reconciliation; it will bring peace to your inner conflict. At this point, you actively and willingly take vision by the hand. You exude an inexplicable confidence that your internal life will no longer be the same, and yet, the places that this process leads will ultimately satisfy all of your internal emotional needs.

FAMILY OF ORIGIN ISSUES
STAGE 1
ONE-WORD DESCRIPTION: **REVIEW**

IS THERE SOMETHING ABOUT ONE'S SELF THAT A PERSON IS NOT AWARE OF?

This Stage is the review of your life (or your client's life) and gives context for why you are interested in pursuing personal change. More specifically, this stage identifies the fundamental concerns, confusions, and frustrations. These issues are likely impacting your personal and/or professional life. To begin, this Stage defines *coping mechanisms* used to deal with life's challenges. Many people try and deal with issues through means they feel are right and effective; they try to cope the best way they can. And when their best efforts do not work, they inevitably feel concerned, confused, frustrated.

This sense of things not working as they should relates to your complex individual beliefs, biases, and/or other ideas you hold to be true. Whenever you experience circumstances or outcomes that fall either inside or outside of these precepts, it is natural to experience feelings that are consistent with these beliefs. In other words, feelings do not appear out of thin air, they are the result of how a person interprets experiences. If things go as expected, we feel vindicated in our beliefs. If thing don't go as expected, we feel that something is wrong or something must be done to make it right.

The way we engage with the world is based on our learned reactions that were likely developed at a young age. The way we think and feel gives rise to the way we behave. These seemingly instinctual responses became *imprinted* because they appeared to have worked, at least when we were young. But as time goes by and life becomes more complicated, as our responsibilities increase, these *coping mechanisms* no longer work.

Still, some people hold on to these behaviors. Others attempt to reject the family of origin values because of disappointment, trauma, or a strong desire to be different or independent. And while this can be good, it can also be part of the confusion and disorientation experienced.

The following statement summarizes this very idea: *A person's persona is a reflection of the expectations placed on them by their family of origin.* The tragedy here is not that you are programmed to think and act in a certain way. Rather, the tragedy exists if you don't evaluate the precepts and adopt workable constructs, ones based on your own unique experiences. When we make informed decisions, we own our own power. We prove that we are living a life of integrity consistent with what truly is, not what we want to be true.

Premeditated ways of handling life issues are numerous and varied. One such mechanism occurs when we feel like exercising control is appropriate because we have been controlled by authority figures in the past. Exercising control over people will always cause them to resist. People rightfully want to exercise their own autonomy. This causes confusion and frustration. In other words, we cause our own pain by not recognizing the futility of what we are doing. We cannot blame others for our feelings of impotence or as justification for the egotism that they were forced to endure. We must take responsibility for our own actions and reactions.

Similarly, techniques like dismissing others who don't adhere to our standards are equally fruitless. Doing so may result from the disdain we felt from our elders, perhaps from differing political, social or religious views. Holding our individuality apart because of a belief in our own rightness yields a judgmental outlook. Separating yourself from that which is outside your personal framework destroys connectedness by causing isolation. In a similar way, requiring that others see issues only in a certain way denies diversity and breeds rigidity. Yet, such complexity exists, and a person's refusal to accept this reality only takes away from others' humanity, reducing them to objects of scorn.

Coming to terms with our individual discordance means also taking ownership of our immaturity, the areas and places in which we need to grow. The purpose of this stage is to open the door to the idea that the person involved (you or your client), the one seeking healing, is part of the problem and therefore can also be part of the solution. Rather than focusing on changing the external world (which is impossible), we need to look inward, asking for help to change ourselves, which is not only possible, but also immensely satisfying. Untangling this Gordian Knot[5] of habits and perceptions is the initial step to gain insight to the internal disorder.

---

5   The Gordian Knot is a Legend of Phrygia Gordium associated with Alexander the Great. It is often used as a metaphor for an intractable problem (disentangling an "impossible" knot) solved easily by a loophole or "thinking outside the box." Wikipedia

A STORY
WHERE FEELINGS OF INADEQUACY CAME FROM

MARSHAL'S FAMILY OF ORIGIN ISSUES

Marshal was born into a well-to-do family with four children. His father was a prominent and successful businessman, loved by his employees and respected in the community. His father was also a tireless lay leader in his faith community, as well as a significant benefactor to the cause. This cause gave him a far-flung reputation for his leadership and generosity.

The father's success was the result of his highly organized, laser-focus ability, which he exhibited effortlessly and took for granted. While his personality was pleasant, he spoke matter-of-factly about those with certain limitations. He minimized them. Some of these people included Marshal's older brother, who had a learning disorder, and Marshal's mother, who was naturally disorganized and who revealed her nervous mannerisms whenever she served her husband.

Marshal revered his father. He had an outgoing personality and because of his older brother's limitation, Marshal took on the role of leader and protector. Yet, he exhibited the same disorganized tendencies and inability to focus as his mother. With a finely tuned sensitivity and empathy, Marshal was subliminally aware of his difficulty measuring up to the father's prowess. This created a disconnect in Marshal's expectations that he too would have the prominence his father possessed, while fueling the underlying belief that he was inadequate.

As Marshal matured and transitioned into adulthood, he attempted to live out his fantasy of recognition and prominence by becoming a minister in the faith in which he grew up. He related well to members of the congregation, but always seemed to be at odds with the leadership of the church. Marshal's tendency to assume a leadership role beyond his station led the church leadership to marginalize him and eventually to relieve him of his pastorate; he lost his marriage as well and was left alone, without moorings. During his demise, Marshal found no support from his father. As a middle-aged man, Marshal was forced to start over without a career, family connections, or self-esteem. He came to hate his father because of feelings of abandonment and rejected his faith out of feelings of resentment, which stemmed from the unreconciled belief that he did not measure up.

Marshal began his process of self-discovery blanketed with layers of unresolved feelings that developed into a debilitating depression. Outwardly pleasant and engaging, Marshal could not shake the guilt he felt; he saw himself as a failure. He blamed his father and the church leaders in order to continue a fantasy of success and prominence.

Until Marshal uncovered and fully understood the web of conflicting issues that began during his formative years, he was unable to let go of the belief that others had taken away his birthright. Because he was unwilling to accept his unrealistic expectations of himself and take responsibility for placing others in roles in an imaginary play where he was the star, he felt abused. Marshal continued in the misery that resulted from the difference between his vision of himself and the reality he faced. All of his reactive feelings were the result of attempting to rewrite history and create a narrative that explained his failure.

Today, armed with a new perspective, Marshal is coming to a place of reality and truth. He continues on the path of self-honesty, appreciating that when old thoughts and reactions surface, they don't need to dominate his acts. This recognition is important for coping with the emotional hangover that stems from his resistance to vanishing into the background. He is embracing the peace that comes from learning to love himself.

Understanding his history and accepting himself has set Marshal free.

EXERCISES FOR STAGE 1:

The answers you provide to the questions below will help define the dynamics present in your nuclear family. If these questions don't address some important aspect of your childhood experience, feel free to add additional material important to your unique experience.

- Write a brief description of your family of origin. How many siblings were present and where did you fall in the ages of the children?

- What were the personality characteristics of the adults and your siblings?

- How would you compare yourself with your parents and siblings?

- How do you feel about the comparison between you and your parents/siblings? (See Feeling Wheel below.[6])

- What were the predominant traits or beliefs you were expected to maintain in order to be acceptable in the family unit? Were

---

6   Robert Plutchik (21 October 1927 – 29 April 2006) was professor emeritus at the Albert Einstein College of Medicine and adjunct professor at the University of South Florida. His research interests include the study of emotions and the study of the psychotherapy process.

you successful or not at meeting these expectations?

- Write a description of situations over which you felt you had little or no control both as a youngster and as an adolescent. These should be situations that occurred frequently and made you feel in a disadvantaged position.

- Explain the types of actions or inactions you took in an attempt to control or mitigate the impact of these situations.

- What actually happened when such mitigation techniques were applied? Did the situation improve or become more difficult?

- How did you feel about yourself, given the results experienced from using these mitigation strategies?

- Review these stories with your coach to understand the full context for these situations.

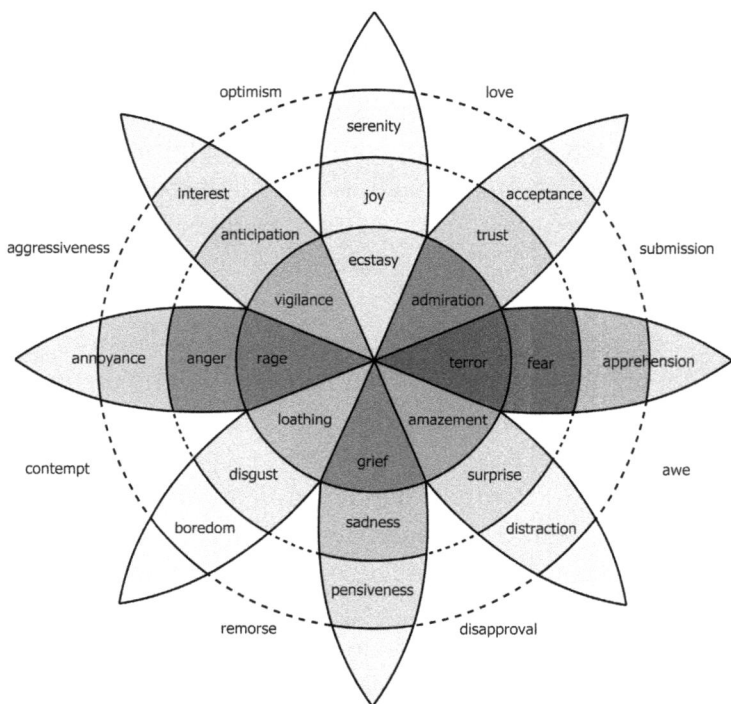

12

RECOGNIZING PERCEPTIONS VS. REALITY
STAGE 2
ONE-WORD DESCRIPTION: **VISION**

HOW DOES RIGIDITY HELP US HOLD ON TO OUR WORLDVIEW?

The objective in Stage 1 was to recognize that our choices have been codified into our perceived reality. This causes a problem, because these beliefs are untrue and conflict with true reality. If we stay isolated in our *"personal core beliefs"* (*the way we understand and react to life issues*), no change will take place. We interpret everything that happens directly or indirectly through the lens of what we believe to be true. Our belief system is reinforced by what we see as evidence that our perceived truth is in fact true. This circular logic leaves us impervious to change.

For example, consider a *Sesame Street* sketch that appeared on the PBS children's program. In the scene, Ernie is standing with Bert, who has a banana in his ear.

> Ernie asks: *"Why do you have a banana in your ear, Bert?"*
> Bert says: *"To keep the alligators away."*
> Astonished, Ernie replies: *"There aren't any alligators on Sesame Street."*
> Bert proudly asserts: *"See, it's working."*

This charming children's story holds an important key to helping us understand why it is difficult to find the change we seek. Each of us carries around a set of beliefs about how life works in our minds. We rarely see them because these beliefs are the filters through which we view and interpret the world. We don't often get a glimpse of these *"erroneous core beliefs"* because we are constantly using them.

To let go of any perceived certainties, we must recognize that we make decisions based on *"(1) incomplete information, (2) unrealistic expectations and (3) erroneous core beliefs."* When we accept these three factors of human nature, we are able also to see that what may have seemed logical might be based on inaccurate premises. We might see also that this causes disconnect between what we believe and what we experience. Each person we interact with has his own set of *"(1) incomplete information, (2) unrealistic expectations and (3) erroneous core beliefs."* Therefore, is it any wonder the numerous opportunities that exist for radical differences of opinions and reactions to the same situation? We experience confusion when we interact with others who see things differently.

Stage 2 involves coming to terms with the possibility that the world is full of contradiction, that a single preconceived set of beliefs is insufficient for coherent clarity. We accept that all things cannot be known, yet remain amazed that somehow the universe functions unabated and unaffected by our trivial attempts to control. Understanding this enables us to see a potential solution, but only when we are open to the possibility that there exists a more meaningful way to live. At this point, we might not know the exact solution, but are confident that it will be revealed.

The following is an illustration of how we can unravel old perceptions to better understand, for example, the source of our anger:

> *"Behind every anger there is a fear,*
> *Behind every fear there is a hurt,*
> *Behind every hurt there is an unmet need,*
> *Behind every unmet need there is a vulnerable child."*

The idea of digging deep into our past and uncovering the traumatic experiences that led to our behaviors can be a painful exercise, and yet, being willing to follow the threads is essential to self-discovery.

Examination and potential change don't require that we must completely discard a *"personal belief system,"* which may have provided a good structure, only to be left with nothing to provide context for our lives. Instead, we are being asked to examine the consequences of our unwavering dedication to these beliefs. Our examination draws a distinction between the essence of the belief and reality. We begin to imagine that if we deal with life (as it actually is), we will begin to experience life differently.

The term *"Erroneous Core Beliefs"* refers to an inaccurate image we have and how we relate to the world. A more general psychological term is Confirmation Bias[7] which is defined as "*the tendency to search for, interpret, favor, and recall information in a way that confirms one's preexisting beliefs or hypotheses, while giving disproportionately less consideration to alternative possibilities. People display this bias when they gather or remember information selectively, or when they interpret it in a Cognitive Bias.*" While these tendencies are common, we are asked here to be aware of this possibility and exhibit a willingness to challenge our preconceived notions.

Another author proposes a unique take on this idea of misperception. Byron Katie[8] states, "*The only time we suffer is when we believe a thought that argues with what is. When the mind is perfectly clear, what is, is what we want. If you want reality to be different than it is, you might as well try to teach a cat to bark. You can try and try, and in the end the cat will look up at you and say, 'Meow.' Wanting reality to be different than it is, is hopeless.*" This is what some refer to as *powerlessness*.

Developing a new perspective isn't instantaneous; rather it takes time and occurs slowly. The incremental nature of settling into a new reality means letting go of our trusted precepts and admitting that we may have incorrectly applied our once strongly held convictions. Once we conceive of being freed from defending our past attitudes, we become more flexible with our choices; life becomes less rigid. We envision that *being*

---

7   The term "confirmation bias" was coined by English psychologist Peter Cathcart Wason (22 April 1924 – 17 April 2003), a cognitive psychologist at University College, London who pioneered the Psychology of Reasoning.
8   Byron Kathleen Mitchell (born December 6, 1942) is an American speaker and author who teaches a method of self-inquiry known as "The Work of Byron Katie."

right brings neither happiness nor acceptance. We recognize that the power we feel by being right, and the resulting attempt to force an opinion, is merely an illusion.

If reality turns out to be different than perception, then we have been living in a fantasy, a form of *insanity.* This may be painful to face, but if we refuse to confront the possibility by examining old patterns, we won't achieve lasting change. The moment we face this dilemma, we also open the door to the fear of change. At the same time, we provide hope that our lives can be lived without conflict. Breaking out of conflict involves a huge intellectual and emotional leap. It is like embarking on an unknown path to an unknown destination, and we must have courage.

A STORY
THE FUTILITY OF SELF-HATRED

BEN'S RECOGNITION OF HIS TRUE REALITY

One of the most important tenets of Ben's family was to present a positive image to the community at large. The appearance of success, leadership, and talent was put on display, primarily so others would associate these characteristics with the family. Ben complied with the family charade. Although he had a slight build, he played football, acted in drama productions, sang in choir groups, and took on a gregarious persona, pushing himself to be the life of the party and to act overly responsible for group activities.

But, the public face did not match what went on in the family behind closed doors or what Ben felt in his private interior. Life inside the home was emotionally confusing, the behavior consistently outside healthy boundaries. Ben seemed to have been singled out as a surrogate husband for his mother. His mother was sexually suggestive to him and brought him into intimate situations that made him extremely uncomfortable. Ben was forced to keep the family secret.

Ben reacted with anger toward women in general and toward himself. As a youngster, he drew pictures of women being mutilated and interpreted his normal attraction to them as being threatening. As Ben grew older, he avoided direct contact with girls and lived in a fantasy world where he remained safe and in control. The dissonance created a dichotomy of being

18

publicly outgoing and inwardly isolated, with deeply buried feelings of guilt and shame.

The social and emotional disorientation that made up Ben's reality was instrumental in his choice of marriage partners. His first wife was a manipulative, emotionally unavailable woman. Soon after the marriage began, she started a long-term affair that produced a second child fathered by her new partner. Because of his learned patterns of behaviors, Ben took on the father role for the child.

The self-hatred that had been broiling under the surface began exhibiting itself in many overt actions. Shoplifting, window peeping, and other antisocial behavior became ways for him to act out. Ben fully expected to be caught to receive the punishment he deserved.

His second marriage was to a single mom, a rage-oholic. This union did not last long, but it served long enough to get Ben into therapy. Even so, he soon got into a third marriage with another emotionally unavailable woman. By this time, Ben had gotten to a point in working on himself to recognize his role in making ineffective decisions and understanding his patterns. Without blaming anyone else, Ben left his dysfunctional marriage and committed to working on himself as his first priority.

With the help of an incest recovery group and long-term therapy, Ben is exploring the reality of his undeserved self-hatred. He is learning to equate his compulsive activities as self-deprivation or forms of self-punishment: his over-commitment to civic responsibilities, intense involvement in theatrical productions, career in commissioned sales, and the resultant financial insecurity and frugality. These decisions have added up to a life he now sees as bouncing from one crisis to another.

His experience in dating and using Internet dating sites serve as a way for him to learn a new pattern of interacting with women while maintaining healthy boundaries. This dating exercise is done in close consultation with his therapist and others to help him sort out true feelings and keep a grasp on his inner reality. Learning not to lose himself in a relationship is critical to not becoming resentful. Being honest about what he wants or doesn't want helps him sort out when a relationship is mutually beneficial. A new sense of self-care is becoming his new reality.

EXERCISES FOR STAGE 2:

These questions attempt to help you uncover how your perceptions differ from the way things really are. The more examples you write about will increase the value of this exercise.

- Prepare a summary description of what you think about yourself, what you assume others think of you, and what evidence you use to draw these conclusions. Complete this exercise for specific periods of time, such as childhood, young adulthood before marriage and after marriage, adulthood after children came along, etc.

- Have there been occasions when others have given you feedback about something you did that seemed out of context in the way you saw the situation? Pick 3-4 occasions for each time period and prepare a narrative for each to flesh out the circumstances, the conflict, the resolution, or lack thereof.

- Summarize when something turned out differently than you thought and discuss why this difference stems from the point of view of your own *personal core beliefs.* ("Beliefs" as used here refers to the criteria used to evaluate your life issues.)

21

- Discuss how you adjusted or did not adjust your understanding of how and why this difference occurred.

- If you did not adjust your thinking, how fiercely did you hold on to your original ideas and what was the consequence of your rigidity?

- How often were these ideas challenged by others, and how did your responses to those challenges change over time?

- Review these thoughts with your coach to explore where these beliefs came from and the impact they had.

MAKING A COMMITMENT
TO REALITY
STAGE 3
ONE-WORD DESCRIPTION: **RESOLVE**

HOW STRONGLY DO YOU WANT TO EXPERIENCE CHANGE?

While Stages 1 and 2 are essential, they are only preparatory for making lasting change. In other words, no change has taken place yet, nor will it take place until and unless a person makes a firm decision. These types of declarations are common. Consider these ritual examples: the presidential inauguration includes an oath to "uphold the Constitution of the United States"; a marriage ceremony involves making a public declaration of one's lifelong dedication; some religious conversions involve a public acknowledgement regarding the authority of a sovereign; Native Americans undertake *"Hambletcha" (a cry for a vision of direction)*. In speaking of living life with sound mental health, Scott Peck[9] defines this commitment as, *"an ongoing process of dedication to reality at all costs."* It is equally important to understand that Stage 3 is a resolution that you will do whatever is necessary to make inner personal change.

This is more than a simple statement; it is a solemn oath to undertake a difficult and even painful process. Think of it as

---

9   M. Scott Peck, an American psychiatrist and best-selling author, best known for his first book, The Road Less Traveled, published in 1978.

the commitment a person makes to climb Mount Everest: the preparation, training, expense and almost superhuman effort, even facing death itself, all of which he experiences alongside an unwavering desire to reach the summit. People don't make a commitment or undertake these types of adventures only to have a few memorable photographs or bragging rights; rather, their purpose is to know internally what they are capable of, to know that they faced a challenge with courage and resolve. After the momentous event, they see themselves differently; they have discovered an inner strength that fundamentally redefines them.

The commitment a person makes to change involves looking at everything making up his personal identity. We are not simply looking for some modest improvements, tweaking around the edges, or identifying some mistakes that were made unwittingly. This involves radical rethinking about how we rationalize and defend our closely held understandings and our behavioral patterns. Changing everything involves a realignment of how we see the structural connections between our inner self and our relationship with ourselves, as well as with the things outside of ourselves. We must remember that *all decisions are imperfect and have unintended consequences,* that we must examine each of our preconceived notions that cause contradiction and replace them with a new presence that transcends the past. And we must do this with no guarantee of what life will look like on the other side.

It may be instructive to read two stories from diverse cultures to better understand these principles. Both stories convey the universality of transformative change. The first is the story of "Jumping Mouse," a Native American legend of a journey from the mundane activities of life to a place (through sacrifice and selflessness) of transcendent beauty and freedom (See Appendix II). The second is "The Fable of the Crescent Moon Bear," a Japanese story about facing fear and deprivation with courage and resolve in order to learn to connect with one's self, as well as with loved ones (See Appendix III).

The vision you obtain in Stage 2 needs to be compelling. It must provide hope that your life will be better, more satisfying, more comfortable. You don't need to know the exact dimensions of what things will look like, only that positive change is possible and that you desire it. Without a positive vision, the commitment I discuss in Stage 3 is likely to be dismissed. You need to know that your investment in this process will pay off.

However, just wanting change isn't enough. Change comes through action and action requires work. Work is a sustained effort requiring tremendous perseverance. Stage 3 is the acknowledgement and acceptance of the effort you will be expending. You must modify your ineffective behaviors, reassess erroneous thought patterns, and reprogram your attitudes. How you act and present yourself in starting down this path is the nature of this commitment. In order to do this, you must viscerally acknowledge the need for change that will permeate your entire being.

A STORY
THE TRAP OF MANIPULATION

STEVE'S COMMITMENT TO INDEPENDENCE

Steve was living a life of fear and confusion; he didn't feel like he fit in. His disorientation had childhood roots, growing up in a small town where he was further isolated with home schooling and within an insular family unit that practiced a self-designed religion. At age 32, Steve decided to live on his own and moved to a nearby city. With little post-secondary education, he worked at a menial job. His future looked dismal, with no direction. Although he had ideas of becoming a nurse, Steve was unable to make the commitment. Nothing seemed to go his way. Instead, Steve felt he was always criticized and blamed by his co-workers and boss, despite giving his job his best effort. He responded by retreating to his apartment and becoming absorbed in pornography, or he returned home to his family where he felt stifled by the demands.

Steve felt like everything that happened to him and to those he loved was out of his control. His siblings were now adults, but dysfunctional. One of his sisters had a child with an abusive man and the relationship ended up in a custody battle. But, she was emotionally unstable and had no support. His other sister had children and still lived with the parents. One of the brothers was barely functional, likely on drugs, and exhibited strange, antisocial behavior.

Both parents possessed their own distorted view of family responsibilities and were severely codependent on one another, as well as on the entire family. Steve was placed in the untenable position of being the adult in the room, trying to resolve the chaos. Whenever he offered support, he felt the futility of his involvement, and when Steve tried to pull away, he was accused of abandoning the family that was so sorely dependent on him. The family manipulated him, accusing him of being uncaring towards his mother and being disrespectful of his father, who was in ill health. The family pleaded with Steve, telling him that he was obligated to support the family. With no place to turn and no refuge in sight, Steve began to numb his feelings; he resigned himself to life without hope.

The change for Steve began without the slightest hint that anything of importance was to come about. By happenstance, Steve met a man who had recently begun his own journey toward self-awareness. During a brief conversation, the man invited Steve to attend a meeting of a group of men who gathered regularly and discussed their unique ways of resolving their inner turmoil. At his first meeting, Steve was astounded. He had never heard stories so like his own. Steven always assumed he was the only person in the world who was condemned to a life of meaningless drudgery. Yet these men seemed to be happy; they appeared to be living by principles that sounded reasonable and doable, they spoke with a wisdom he had never heard, they welcomed him and told him he did not have to face life alone.

This initial event was only the beginning of what Steve would later deem a lifelong pursuit for happiness and freedom. After a time of self-reflection and with the help of a few of the men (whom he now calls friends), Steve gained clarity on his attitude of resignation. He saw that his negativity and despair were walls of a prison he alone had erected. Most important, Steve realized he had the power to set himself free.

In a single act of self-preservation and independence, Steve signed up for a tour of duty in the U.S. military with plans to become a medic and make a career of service to his country. The day of his decision, Steve called his friends, beaming with excitement and pride. It was a day to mark in red on the calendar—the first day of his new life. Over the years, Steve has maintained contact with his friends and speaks of them as the new, loving and supportive family he chose.

Life in the service is not without challenges and uncertainty, but now Steve has a self-directed purpose and direction.

EXERCISES FOR STAGE 3:

These questions address the idea of change that has happened in your life and how you adjusted to change. These experiences will help you make a commitment to additional change.

- Identify a time when you experienced an event that fundamentally changed your circumstances or the way you looked at life. For example: you got or lost a job, you got married or got divorced, a child was born, a family member died, you had a religious conversion, you suffered a debilitating accident. These types of events changed the way you saw and/or reacted to the world.

- Discuss how you responded to the change, both immediately and in the long run.

- Was there a plan or commitment involved in adjusting to new circumstances or did the change take place by happenstance? Discuss the transformation(s) in terms of attitudinal change.

- Write a brief description of what you want for your inner life and why. Possible concepts to explore may include better self-esteem, clearer direction, a more positive outlook, or more satisfying relationships with more empathy, etc.

- In the past, have you attempted these types of changes?

- If so, how did it work out; for example, when you implemented an approach to bring about change did things get better, worse or stay the same?

- Why do you think you got the outcome you experienced?

- If you could plan for change, how would you go about it?

- Review your outlook with your coach. Classify your thoughts in terms of practicality, attainability, and importance. Identify which objectives are accomplishments and which are fundamental personal change.

PHASE II: DISCOVERY

DISCOVERY is defined in Stages 4 through 9 as we learn to face ourselves without masks, without excuses, without blaming others, without bravado or martyrdom. This unadulterated and comprehensive self-assessment is the opportunity for a person to stand naked on stage in an auditorium full of spectators. Although frightened and embarrassed, we know we have nothing left to hide; rather, we request acceptance for who we are, not for who we pretend to be. At the end, you will look back at this discovery as exhilarating, as freeing.

Stage 4 is known by some to be similar to an *inventory* exercise. The term inventory suggests a complete accounting, item by item, of what is currently on the shelf. An inner personal inventory is no less detailed. Stages 1 through 3 began the process with a general overview. Stage 4 is both rigorous in its clarity and exhaustive in its completeness of character traits and behaviors.

Stage 5 takes a summary of the information developed in Stage 4 to some trusted confidants as an act of transparency. If a person were to prepare this material and not share it with others, the information could not become real. Sharing the information with others to bear witness demonstrates your inner strength, the commitment necessary to continue forward.

Stage 6 puts quantitative values on the items listed in the inventory. The gravity of the cumulative costs of a person's behaviors is easily avoided if this Stage is too vague. Numbers are real and provide a measure of where you have placed emphasis in your life choices.

Stage 7 may be considered the center-point, the fulcrum where inner personal change begins to take place. The commitment you made in Stage 3 to seek change comes to fruition here. In a supreme act of humility, you surrender your enumerated behavioral characteristics; however, change does not take place until you ask for help in completing the process. I have included a discussion of what "help" means as it relates to this section.

Stage 8 is more expansive. Stage 4 is a detailed review of how your actions and behaviors have impacted you. Here, behaviors are assessed as seen by others. The focus becomes empathy. This Stage deals with the broad range of social interactions. Specific incidents may come to mind, but you are looking to enumerate general categories of people who experience your immature behavior.

Stage 9 is similar but concentrates more specifically on people with whom you have a long-term and close relationship. In addressing your interactions with these people, the inventory from Stage 4 becomes helpful. The information provides substance to the inappropriateness of your style. Taking responsibility for your self-centered behaviors in situations where loved ones have been affected is coupled with a definition of the change that others can expect from you in the future.

Discovery implies finding something not previously known and typically requires help from others who understand the process. This process is designed to uncover inner personal realities that you previously ignored or misrepresented. However, discovery also implies experimentation. You must work within the elements of your life to see different cause-and-effect reactions to various stimuli. Like science, a theory may be accurate, but until proven through experimentation, the theory holds little value. Once experiments provide observable evidence that shows predictability, industrial-scale applications become possible. The science analogy is not meant to imply mathematical precision, but rather to remind you that science and discovery involve trial and error; some unexpected turns take place and additional questions are raised, all before clarity presents itself. But, as you make incremental progress, a new self emerges.

Discovery is the development of a complete and unvarnished picture of a person's self. Some people resist undergoing such in-depth discovery because they refuse to see themselves negatively, or as being dishonest. It is crucial that this interpretation be dispelled, because no judgment should be placed on what was previously unseen. Without an honest assessment of your true characteristics, you remain blind to your *core beliefs*, lost in a labyrinth of misperceptions.

COMPARING COMPETING REALITIES IN TERMS OF BEHAVIOR
STAGE 4
ONE-WORD DESCRIPTION: **HONESTY**

HOW DO YOU ACT WHEN YOU WANT ONE THING, BUT RECEIVE SOMETHING DIFFERENT?

This Stage has a very practical orientation. Regardless of perceptions, beliefs, rights and wrongs or any other cognitive interpretations, there is concrete clarity in what a person does. A person's real actions are undeniable. And, it is equally certain that their actions resulted in real consequences. In Stage 4, accepting reality includes taking responsibility for your actions and their impact. First, it requires cataloging your behaviors and taking a hard look at how extensively they exhibit your attitudes, thought processes, decisions, and resulting actions. We gain clarity once we accept reality.

Stage 4 is the development of a complete review of both positive and negative personal characteristics. The underlying nature of these behaviors has been internalized and rationalized and thereby can be difficult to recognize. This means that we lapse into perpetual self-delusion about our roles, about what we feel entitled to obtain or what we expect from others. In this case, there are two steps in making an inventory. First, we take stock of specific behaviors and the long-term consequences of the behaviors. Secondly, we translate our actions into the underlying motivations that give rise to identified behaviors.

36

The thoroughness of this list is vital because it forms the basis for what will follow next in this process. The list is used in Stage 5 to acknowledge our true nature to others. The list provides the outline we will use to count the cost of our behavior in Stage 6. The list identifies those elements of our personality that need to change in Stage 7. The list is essential in Stage 8 as well, to comprehend exactly how these behaviors have impacted others. And in Stage 9, the list supports the formulation of a new behavior set.

Competing realities are suggested to provide the sense that what we see as our perceived reality is likely different than the reality experienced by others. You are asked to explore the tension that exists between these two forms of awareness. We tend to see vividly what we want and react negatively when we don't get it. Rather than adjusting to the true reality, we maneuver, manipulate, or argue to change reality to what we desire. This typically leads to experiencing disappointment and frustration.

Consider a management consulting exercise (not unlike an "*intervention*" where a family confronts a loved one who has some form of addiction) that helps individuals achieve a better understanding of themselves within the context of the functioning business. Three steps are used:

1. A member of a department (the subject individual) is given a set of questions that define his performance as an employee and is asked to rate himself as being a valuable team member.

2. The subject individual is asked to rate how
    others in the department would rate his value.

3. Then, each of the other members in the
    department is asked to anonymously rate
    the value of the subject individual.

When the subject individual reviews the full set of answers regarding himself, he begins to see the unadulterated reality of the impact of his behavior. The most important information in this exercise is what others think, because it gets us out of our self-protection mode and forces a new perspective. We begin to see how our actions affect others and how we impact our own value in the situation. There is power in being forced out of denial and shown evidence of the consequences of our actions.

Here the purpose is to achieve a new level of honesty concerning the real cause and effect in your life. Most people don't consider these connections and, if confronted in a nonclinical environment, will likely not accept the true reality. The task to characterize and classify your behavior is both difficult and painstaking. This phase cannot be done without commitment, courage, and nonjudgmental support so that you are not forced to see yourself as bad. Rather, you will come to understand that you were simply unaware of the impact of your behavior.

A STORY
RECOGNIZING MISPLACED LOYALTY

JONATHON HAD SEEN HIS LIFE THROUGH AN IDEALIZED PRISM, UNTIL HE DIDN'T

By all outward appearances, Jon was a fine person. A retired professional, he was known in the community for his honest dealings and civic involvement. He had been born into that community and grew up being friends with many of those who were now movers and shakers within the power structure. He raised his family to be responsible adults, showing his love for them and a growing brood of grandchildren with doting affection.

Yet on a personal level, Jon's life wasn't working. His relationship with his wife had, for the last 30-plus years, been sterile, contentious. He and his wife had slept in separate bedrooms for three decades and she constantly tried to control and dominate him. Jon accepted his unhappiness as though it were background noise. Being an intellectual, he rationalized his situation as a character test and the lack of intimacy as a normal part of aging.

However, in previous years, Jon had been drawn into a sexual affair that itself was unsatisfying due to the lack of the emotional connection he craved. Everything about the affair had been antithetical to his ideals and he could not reconcile his actions. Instead of getting in touch with his inner feelings about his life, Jon minimized the affair, deeming it an interesting milestone in his life's journey.

The affair did not remain a secret. After being confronted by his wife, Jon began therapy and haltingly began facing the reality of his unhappiness. His wife continually used the affair as a bludgeon to drive a wedge between him and the children. Still, Jon showed little effort to redefine his self-image. He kept his role in the family as leader, protector, and provider.

He held on to the idea that his worth was defined by the father role. That role had been appropriate when his children were still under his care, and he had done that job admirably well. He began to recognize that circumstances were now different and that old perceptions were no longer valid. This was the beginning of a redefinition of his responsibilities within the family. The change came neither easily nor quickly.

He had long contemplated getting a divorce even though he was in his seventies, and he knew that the financial impact of such a move would be great. To avoid confronting himself, Jon attempted to engage his wife in discussing the nature of their relationship. She provided no satisfactory acknowledgement that his needs to feel safe or worthy were even relevant. Instead, she repeatedly berated and belittled him without mercy. And he took the abuse with debilitating stoicism.

Jon sought legal advice, and intended to communicate with the adult children the nature of irreconcilable differences he had with their mother. He drafted a letter that he could send to family members to express the need to establish an independent relationship that circumvented his wife's interference. But he resisted sending the letter; Jon wasn't yet ready to change his perception of his responsibility.

Then it happened. While away visiting his children, Jon's wife rifled through his things in his private bedroom and discovered evidence of his communication with the divorce lawyer, the draft letter to the children, and other writings. Jon finally embraced his anger and could wait no longer. In a totally antiseptic way, they agreed to divorce and began breaking up the household. Whether by choice or force, Jon is now ready to face his true reality. Slowly he is embracing new actions that reflect a mature understanding of previously held beliefs that were based on misrepresentations and an unrealistic self-image.

EXERCISES FOR STAGE 4:

- Break your life into 10-year increments. For each segment, list those things you did that you are proud of and those things that had negative outcomes when you thought they were going to be successful.

- Write a summary of your motivations in these situations and how you treated others with respect to the outcomes.

THINGS I'M PROUD OF	THINGS WITH NEGATIVE OUTCOMES
(ADD LINES AS NECESSARY)	

- For the same 10-year increments, think of typical and recurring events that left you feeling angry, fearful, resentful, or confused. Make a separate table for each feeling (anger, fear, resentment and confusion), filling out the table with the specific events with detail about your internal reaction (not the outside forces that caused the reaction). In this exercise, Long Term Consequences refer to the fundamental personality traits that resulted from chronic behavior.

EVENT	FEELING	BEHAVIOR	LONG-TERM CONSEQUENCE
(ADD LINES AS NECESSARY)			

Questions regarding personality characteristics and behavior

The table below is to be completed three times.

1. How does the subject person rate himself?
2. How does the subject person think others would rate him?
3. How does each of the other team members rate the subject person?

Subject Person:

CHARACTERISTIC OF VALUE TO THE TEAM	ABOVE AVERAGE			BELOW AVERAGE	
	EXTREMELY	SOMEWHAT	AVERAGE	SOMEWHAT	EXTREMELY
FOCUSES ON TEAM GOALS					
MEETS GOALS ON TIME					
LISTENS TO OTHERS					
DOES A FAIR SHARE OF WORK					
IS POSITIVE AND SUPPORTIVE					
THINKS CREATIVELY					
WORKS INDEPENDENTLY					
TAKES OWNERSHIP OF TASKS					
TAKES OWNERSHIP OF RESULTS					
(ADD LINES AS NECESSARY)					

(The way this exercise is written represents a work situation, but the questions can be revised for other situations such as family or any working group)

Make a list of your personal characteristics that you feel describe the real you in such a situation.

Review this list with your coach to refine these personal characteristics or personality traits.

The following material was adapted from a publication by the Los Angeles, California city schools in their educational program. The statements define attitudes that people with characteristics of mature adults tend to exhibit.

A CHECKLIST FOR EVALUATING MATURITY

1. Does not automatically resent criticism because a suggestion for improvement is contained therein.
2. Recognizes that self-pity is futile and childish – a way of transferring the blame or disappointments onto others.
3. Does not lose one's temper readily or fly off the handle about trifles.
4. Is rational in moments of stress, dealing with them in a logical fashion.
5. Accepts responsibility for his own actions and decisions and does not blame others when things go wrong.
6. Accepts reasonable delays without impatience, realizing that one must adjust himself or herself to the convenience of others.
7. Is a good loser, accepts defeat and disappointment without complaint or poor sportsmanship.
8. Does not worry unduly about things that cannot be changed.
9. Does not boast or show off, but when praised or complimented, accepts it with grace and

appreciation and without false modesty.
10. Applauds others' achievements with sincere good will.
11. Rejoices in the good fortune and success of others, having outgrown petty jealousy and envy.
12. Is not overly argumentative in discussions with others, thinking others must accept their point of view.
13. Listens courteously to the opinions of others, even those holding opposing views.
14. Does not find fault with every little thing or criticize those who do things differently.
15. Makes reasonable plans for activities and tries to carry them out in an orderly fashion.
16. Does not do things on the spur of the moment without due consideration.

Read each statement and prepare a written statement of how you feel your reactions and attitudes reflect your personal level of maturity.

Reflect on how you feel your acquaintances might describe your personality.

Review your perceptions with the coach to get feedback and consider any refinements that may be appropriate.

ACKNOWLEDGING MISPERCEPTIONS AND UNPRODUCTIVE BEHAVIOR
STAGE 5
ONE-WORD DESCRIPTION: **INTEGRITY**

HOW DO WE REMAIN TRUE TO OURSELVES?

The work that took place in Stage 4 has been introspective. The effort to pull together cause and effect has been illuminating and provides us with a new sense of how the daily dynamics of our life unfold. However, this exercise is not complete until we get this information out of our minds and into the objective world. Therefore, the purpose of Stage 5 is to get objective feedback in order to have a realistic assessment of ourselves.

We prepare a cogent summary of how we have acted in the past, including the motivations that have unwittingly driven us to act in artless ways. We then relate the nature of our behavioral patterns and the experiences of unintended consequences to a select group. This is not an indictment of what we have done; it isn't "*right or wrong.*" Rather, this stage classifies our behaviors as either productive or unproductive, and acknowledges the extent to which our repeated actions have formed our personas.

The purpose of this stage is to divulge personal information and insight to others, but in a measured way. First, we pick a few close and nonjudgmental acquaintances to listen and provide feedback on how we see ourselves. You might choose teachers, counselors, clergy, human resources professionals, and the like. These confidants are likely to give reasoned feedback and emphasize the full range of your personality characteristics. Doing so is beneficial because it tempers a personal view with a perspective of what others see. This process ensures that we form an accurate, objective narrative of ourselves.

This act of accountability is like the exercise in the preceding section where members of a work team evaluated one another. In this case, there exists more opportunity for a well-rounded perception of one's personality traits to come to the forefront. Situations including work, social, family and other such interactions are places where our attitudes and behaviors are on display. As we develop awareness of our interaction style, we begin to understand how our own behaviors affect ourselves, as well as our social environments.

Attitudes are important in that personality traits affect the quality of interaction, but actions are much easier to recognize and address than attitudes. If we change behavior and then the attitudes, others will likely reassess our attitudes automatically. Therefore, it is more beneficial to catalog our observable acts. When we evaluate the ways our behaviors affect our social interaction and acknowledge them without shame or guilt, we are embracing our humanity.

Consider the example from the movie *The Horse Whisperer,* starring Robert Redford. In the story, the characters came to see their internal selves by being exposed to totally different worldviews. The characters have focused so much of their lives on their external world that they have lost sight of their true feelings. Their humanness was obscured by fear, isolation, and the need to succeed. Their internal selves came into focus as they witnessed the horse responding to gentleness. As humans, they too responded physically to the subtle invitation to reconnect.

Here I emphasize assessing behaviors rather than making moral judgments. In this application, we view behaviors as unrecognized habits that, once discovered, generate a desire to modify them. Avoiding guilt and shame with their implication of unacceptability eliminates any obstacle that may otherwise be difficult to overcome. The application of accountability in this process is to learn how to have better relationships withourselves and others, and improve our self-worth.

The act of exposing our actions to others and inviting them to comment on how these behaviors have affected our interactions with them is essential for change to take place. We can't be willing to have this openness if not for our desire to change, or the commitment made in Stage 3. The act of bringing others into our discovery fulfills the requirements of honesty, integrity, and humility that I laid out previously. We demonstrate honesty when we expose the whole unvarnished truth about ourselves. We demonstrate integrity when we make no excuses or rationalizations for what we now know to be true. And we demonstrate humility when our expression of this truth allows us to take responsibility for our obvious behavior.

A STORY
AN UNRECOGNIZED BLIND SPOT

SAMUEL'S CERTAINTY OF WHAT IS GOOD AND RIGHT

Samuel is a good and decent person. He is generous, has personal integrity, dedication to his faith, is friendly and outgoing, and possesses a gift for capturing people's attention. He is serious when showing a willingness to be of service on his terms, whenever the situation presents itself. These characteristics have led to his financial success. During his school years, Sam was academically outstanding. In his early professional years, he was a top real estate salesperson, always receiving laudatory recognition and promotions. Samuel then became an investor, showing his uncanny ability to make deals.

These accomplishments are very important to Sam. During conversations, Sam is quick to point out that he is the best at whatever he undertakes: the best student that knows more than the teacher, the best salesman with abilities unmatched by his peers, the best deal-maker who negotiates in a way to outwit all parties, the best Christian through an understanding of scripture with the best application of this understanding, and the best lover as related by his many wives. Samuel is always the best.

Given his gregarious nature, Sam is totally at ease in any social situation and often gathers a crowd around him, likely due to his dominant personality. He jokes easily with everyone

51

he meets, interrupting any ongoing conversation to greet a stranger. Community leaders associate with him because of his seemingly wide sphere of influence. Yet, Sam does not realize that these friendships, although numerous, are actually very shallow. Samuel admits that there are very few people he can call a real friend, and even then, those relationships lack emotional intimacy. He is content to remain in his self-righteous cocoon.

In the face of personal crisis, Samuel made an effort to deal with inner personal issues. Sam undertook this self-examination, feeling motivated to prove he could excel at this as well. He talked about how he took over the responsibility for the family when his father passed away before he was an adolescent. He recalled that he felt totally detached from his own family, particularly his wife. He readily acknowledged he had direct conversations with God. He spoke of the results on personality tests that show his prowess as a Type A leader, not an implementer, for that would require him to work with others.

Samuel justified his behavior recalling an incident in business, where he and a partner split because he was unwilling to compromise on inconsequential administrative issues. Sam was unwilling to see his part in a situation with his faith congregation, where he was both a member and on the church board, that became untenable because of his rigidity. He gave little thought about dismissing his last wife because she would not follow his advice and direction.

A lack of empathy is at the base of Sam's problem. Having divorced the mother of his children, he continues to interact with her in a quasi-family mode. Even though Sam lives alone, he participates in holiday activities with her and the children, as if it were normal. He implies that these behaviors are evidence of his nobility, not a manifestation of his lack of feelings. He takes perverse pride in this bizarre relationship that is more robotic than human.

When confronted about his self-contained world, Sam becomes angry, claiming, "*I can't change and I won't consider things that don't come to me naturally because there is nothing I can do about them.*" Sam is content with his myopic view where nothing can penetrate his protective shield. He sees only what he wants to see, is content in his perceived success, and discusses only those things that enhance his self-image. Without breaking through his misperceptions and unproductive behavior, his self-image remains opaque and change is not possible. Being unable to receive feedback from others leaves Sam unable to get out of his own way.

EXERCISES FOR STAGE 5:

This set of exercises is designed to bring transparency to your work thus far.

- Prepare a summary that you will use with the people you want to hear your story. This summary may be in the form of a letter sent before the meeting. It could also be a list of bullet-points you use to speak extemporaneously.

- Make a list of persons with whom you can make these disclosures. They should not be family members, people with whom you have had an intimate relationship or people with an ax to grind from past interaction. They are people who know you and who will give you objective feedback, and not divulge what you say or use the information against you.

- Review this list with your coach to select 4 to 6 individuals with whom to have this conversation.

- Make an appointment with each one so a face-to-face conversation can take place. If such people are at some distance, arrangements for an interview using the phone or SKYPE can be made.

- Conduct such meetings with the positive expectation that you will come away with an expanded and objective view of yourself.

- Write a thank-you note to each evaluator, identifying a specific insight you received.

- Write a complete summary of each meeting with equal weight given to your positive characteristics as well as those that are problematic.

- Review these summaries with your coach and discuss both what you confirmed about yourself and new information you had not considered before.

- Take time to reflect on and write about the extent to which your actions have affected yourself and others.

- Write a description of the feelings engendered by these revelations.

- Review all the material with your coach and compose a list of the specific behavior traits that define you.

COUNTING THE COSTS
STAGE 6
ONE-WORD DESCRIPTION: **ASSESSMENT**

HOW MUCH DO PAST BEHAVIORS COST A PERSON OVER A LIFETIME?

Both Stages 4 and 5 deal with behaviors and consequences, but Stage 6 is a specific attempt to come to terms with the extent to which our actions cause us to hurt ourselves by misrepresenting reality. Did you mistakenly blame others for a divorce, an affair, job loss, a habitual indulgence or missed opportunity? The common denominator in these situations and events is your individual choices and involvement. Taking stock of your own part is necessary to put such inappropriate justification to rest. More important, an honest assessment brings us to the inescapable thought that we must seek change.

Consider a man whose feelings are hurt when he is passed over for job advancement. He reads the paper after getting to work, takes an extra-long lunch and leaves work early. Over a year or several years, how much in time, in terms of dollars, has he stolen from his employer? How has his attitude affected the morale of others to whom he confides his dark humor? How many potential other opportunities has he missed due to his lack of enthusiasm and active participation? If he faces reality head-on, he will see the damage he has inflicted on himself by his negativity and blaming of others.

Or, consider a man who loves playing golf, spending weekends on the course, spending time with his buddies in the clubhouse after a round, buying new clubs and accessories. He even plans vacations around his hobby, with little thought to his wife and family. I am not suggesting that having a hobby is inappropriate, but that we need to assess if an activity is an enjoyable pastime or a way to circumvent dealing with relationships that might be difficult. If we are clear about our internal turmoil and our desire to circumvent the conflict, we will likely experience a need to make things right.

Up to this point in this process, the idea of change may have been recognized, but acknowledged as merely prudent or praiseworthy. We tell ourselves messages to minimize and justify our behaviors. "All people can make improvements, I know I'm not perfect."

"Everybody does it, I'm not that bad" is a common theme. The content in this stage is not a superficial review, but an in-depth assessment of consequential effects that impact the very core of a person.

This is the moment we begin the process of change. This is where the commitment we made in Stage 3 begins to engage us fully in the mechanics of actual change. It is as if we are standing in an open field, facing east, just before sunrise. We see a pale light in the sky that grows brighter, illuminating the clouds with an incandescent glow, followed by a burst of blinding light. This is the moment where change really comes into focus. Those who have experienced this internal sunrise report feelings of urgency in their need for change, a sense of being repulsed by the identified behaviors that defined their patterns of interaction with themselves and others.

In quantitative terms, facing reality impacts a person's psyche. How much money have we unnecessarily spent, how much time have we wasted, how many relationships have we damaged or lost, how many of our dreams have been dashed? The accumulated costs over a lifetime of repeated self-centered, self-righteous and self-indulgent behavior result in real costs. Many people on this path have indulged in this type of dishonesty with justification and excuses. With a quantitative sense of reality, we see the efficacy of change with a stark reality that we might not have otherwise.

Stage 6 is an essential step to fundamental transformative change. Stages 1 through 5 are the foundation on which we come to a dramatic disinterment of our personality. Stage 6 is where the vision and hope of the process are captured in the deepest part of our inner being. We confront all the misinterpretation, the subterfuge and outright lying and strip it away so we can see reality more clearly.

Change doesn't take place just because there is an awareness, regardless of the magnitude of the cost; rather, change takes place only when we experience a new imperative. Almost as if we see the picture hidden in the optical illusion, we see our unadulterated behavior for the first time, and we desire to be transported away from that which now seems unthinkable. It's hard to describe this intense emotional experience we have during this stage, but many people report a compelling power without which any change at all would be limited and transitory. We desire this new inner self because it is more attractive, more appealing, and more peaceful. And we cannot help but want to adopt change.

A STORY
RECOGNIZING WHEN TO STOP RUNNING

DONALD'S MOMENT OF CLARITY CONCERNING THE COSTS

There is a lot that is unconventional about Donald. He lives with a unique and well-developed social camouflage that helps him stand out as a sensitive artistic soul. Getting to know Donald is a challenge because he is constantly attempting to deflect the focus by using self-deprecating humor to keep the conversation off balance. However, Don is a deep thinker, smart, well read, and, with the help of several caring men, has spent many years in exploring his motivations, attitudes, and behaviors.

Don grew up like most, in a situation that he couldn't comprehend or rationalize. His family was well entrenched as upper mid-westerners rooted in their community. Don attended the Catholic school in the primary grades where, in the sixth grade, he had an abusively strict nun for a teacher. Don was repeatedly hit with a yardstick and punished in front of the class; however, he wasn't able to tell his parents because of their devout faith. Instead he suffered in silence, stifling his anger in isolation.

By age 14, Don knew he did not belong in that time and space and began to contemplate his escape. The vivid memory he has of this awakening is excruciatingly poignant as it demonstrates his loneliness.

"The snow was falling softly as I stood in the alley entrance, under a lone street lamp, across from the house where I lived. The dim light in the windows against the silhouette of the house was not inviting, only a reminder of being awkwardly out of place. Other than that, I had an absence of feelings but a certainty that this existence was unbearable and came with a deep resignation. I knew I was lost and alone with no safe place to go. I trusted no one and knew no one who would help or even understand my deep embarrassment.

I had been taking drugs for some time but the escape they provided was only temporary. I considered running away, not to a particular place, but away from this place where I experienced only pain and confusion. Shivering in the cold I resolved to go. I did not know where, when or how but I was determined to change, because if I did not go I would die."

By age 16, Don was on the road, deep into drugs. He did whatever was necessary to survive. He lived on the street, staying only a short time in any one place. Eventually, in his twenties, Don found himself in Montana, where he created an existence using primitive skills he had learned from other societal dropouts. This was illegal, but he didn't care. He was little more than another animal in the forest, but this new lifestyle gave him the opportunity to hone his survival skills, giving him an abiding love of nature.

In a moment of serendipity, Don found Narcotics Anonymous. With unrepentant anger, he railed against any established order. He set himself apart, a nonconformist, a desperado, a rebel, an antagonist of anything that resembled establishment. Yet, without understanding why, he stuck with the recovery program, remaining sober, finishing a bachelor's degree, and grudgingly became more civilized. But, Don still had one foot out the door.

His tendency to run was apparent in his first two marriages. When faced with difficulties, or when he felt threatened or had a sense of potential abandonment, Don pulled up stakes and disappeared. Living in small mountain towns and surrounding himself with other dysfunctional characters, he drifted from one dead-end situation to another, paying the price that resistance to change extracted. Yet he never gave up.

In his fifties, Don became a pillar in the NA recovery community. Married again, Don is forced to face his vulnerability, but resists the urge to run because he knows and is able to care for himself. He accepts the costs he paid because of poor choices, and chooses to live with his past without being held captive by it.

EXERCISES FOR STAGE 6:

- Based on traits developed in Stage 4, count the costs such traits have incurred over the time they have been present. Use numbers and include the combination of dollars and time if both apply. Consider the following tables to aid calculations:

Dollars Spent

Activity	Unit Cost/Incident	Number of Incidents/ elapsed time	Total Incidents	Unit Cost x Total Incidents
(Add lines as necessary)				

Time Spent

Activity	Unit Cost/Incident	Number of Incidents/ elapsed time	Total Incidents	Unit Cost x Total Incidents
(Add lines as necessary)				

Opportunities Lost

Potential Opportunity	Opportunity that was Lost	Dollar Value of Opportunity	Total Opportunities	Total Dollars Lost
(Add lines as necessary)				

Relationships Damaged or Lost

Potential Relationships	Reason the Relationship was Lost	Total Relationships Lost
(Add lines as necessary)		

- Were you surprised at the cumulative amount of these calculations? Describe your feelings of loss.

- Describe the strength of your conviction to make inner personal change.

- What will you do with the resources that will become available once change takes place?

- Identify the extent to which the new activities will be exciting and satisfying to your life.

- Review these calculations with your coach.

THE AGENT OF CHANGE
STAGE 7
ONE-WORD DESCRIPTION: **HUMILITY**

WHAT IS IT INSIDE US THAT ALLOWS CHANGE TO TAKE PLACE?

It's common in contemporary culture to see the need for change and to make change happen, in order to improve things. There is a feeling of power in being recognized for accomplishments, intelligence, or winning. We idealize these feelings in modern society, but they likely stem from the same impulses that cause us difficulties in the first place. When we attempt to take control of every problem, we are acting out of self-will. Seeing our place in the world from this old vantage point precludes being open; it runs counter to our sense of being a small part of life. With a new approach, we come to recognize the uncontrollable complexity of situations.

Rather than taking charge, Stage 7 explores the idea of "*surrender.*" Surrender (which is synonymous with humility) is acknowledging that our past impulsive actions were counterproductive and that a new attitudinal approach will yield better outcomes. It becomes clear that, without surrendering, change is difficult if not impossible.

It is important for us to understand what surrender is not. Surrender is not passive. It's not giving up, nor is it humiliation. Humiliation requires us to admit to losing, or to having been wrong, which happens when we assume we are right in the first place. Similarly, surrender is not negotiable, or for that matter, re-negotiable. Surrender is the recognition that all we assumed to be true is not, and that we must accept our new and different reality from this point forward.

Humility is being open to making positive change because something new has come to light. Surrender is relinquishing the idea that we are better than or superior to others and that the outside world must submit to our will. Humility puts our contributions into perspective, allowing us to give others credit for their role in resolution and moving forward together. Humility is living *in* reality.

Consider the Merriam-Webster dictionary definition of humility: *"The quality or state of not thinking that you are better than other people."* A central element of humility is to refocus our attention on the *"we"* in a situation rather than the *"I."* The driving power resides outside ourselves in the goodwill of the many, which is immensely greater than what the single individual possesses. Being willing to accept the premise that the combined power beyond our personal motivation is present and will act beneficially on behalf of the composite interests—this is the real test of humility. The acceptance of something other than our own consciousness is profoundly life changing and resides at the highest order of human expression.

Here we notice a dichotomy. We may have been taught that putting others' needs ahead of our own is an act of humility, and yet this can lead to expectations as to how the other person will or should respond. A school of modern psychology deals with this in the study of codependency.[10] This idea supposes that, if I do something for you, you will do something I want you to do. I apply an alternative principle, which is, *"If one does what is right for oneself, it is the right thing for all involved in a situation."* If the mindset is to be our authentic self in a situation and to accept the outcome without trying to manipulate a result, then this isn't a selfish way to deal with others. Humility doesn't mean that we need to sublimate or lose ourselves to others, but rather that we should maintain our integrity without trying to dominate or control the situation.

Humility is also asking for help. Asking for help from others has obvious benefits. When we examine the benefits of asking for help, it appears to be easy for people in subservient positions. However, it is also a powerful tool for those coming from a position of strength. Those who admit to needing help and have the capacity to accept it show humility, not weakness.

Here a tricky question is posed in the discussion. Who are we asking for help? Is the invocation directed to a supreme being, a positive energy in the universe, the composite wisdom of a trusted group? *"For those who have a working concept of a higher power this question is already answered. For those with no concept or a negative, distrustful view of such issues, no amount of logic or argument to believe will help bring this concept into focus."*

---

10   According to specialist Lennard J. Davis, the concept of codependence "comes directly out of Alcoholics Anonymous, part of a dawning realization that the problem was not solely that of the addict, but also the family and friends who constitute a support network for the alcoholic."

For those of us for whom it is difficult to imagine a *power greater than ourselves* to bear as part of our humility, it is suggested that we wait and we hold this question until later in the process. After we have experienced positive changes for which we can't provide a rational explanation, we might view things differently. Belief in a traditional God isn't a requirement, rather only that we have an inner confidence that "*we will be taken care of.*" We don't need to worry about how this happens. The benefits from this process don't come because we accept a spiritual idea; they come because we choose to see change as a gift and humbly accept it.

A STORY
IT'S NOT ANYONE'S FAULT

GERRY'S DISCOVERING THE POWER IN SURRENDER

Gerry couldn't remember a time he didn't feel defeated. The option of suicide was his constant companion and he was chronically depressed. Life was an endless stream of disappointments, existing in shades of dark foreboding gray.

Gerry grew up in an upper-middle-class family with an older brother and sister and a younger brother. His mom was needy and whiny, while his dad was domineering. His siblings adopted a competitive approach where scores were kept for a lifetime. The struggle of "one-upmanship" was constant and unrelenting. His parents divorced and taking care of his mom became Gerry's full-time job. Although no one assigned him the duty, he willingly took it on. The position gave him the potential for recognition and self-worth, but the torment from his siblings seemed even more devastating.

A profound and biting resentment grew in Gerry's gut, crying out for vindication and justice. Into his adulthood, Gerry attempted to rewrite his story internally by confronting his virtual siblings, attempting to prove his worth and value. His private narrative seemed righteous and logical, so why did he break down in tears every time his underlying insecurities were exposed? Gerry's unwillingness to face his tormentors directly meant he would not be relieved of the impotence he felt each and every day.

Gerry was demonstrably intelligent, quick to pick up new knowledge and skills, and hardworking, yet he couldn't seem to keep a job. There was a hard edge to his interaction with co-workers and supervisors that included accusatory tones and condescending attitudes. To avoid conflict and embarrassment, he began operating independently by doing contract work in his chosen industry. This option provided some protection for his ego, but kept him isolated and trapped in his internal struggles.

Gerry wanted to feel the way he imagined others felt about themselves. He read self-help books, engaged in therapy over many years, and sought absolution from his pastor, but nothing could shake his self-loathing. Alternatively, Gerry secretly engaged in many forms of self-indulgence including compulsive masturbation, cross-dressing, and driving aimlessly around seedy neighborhoods where he could pick up street prostitutes. Yet he couldn't bring himself to consummate these activities, out of fear that something bad and out of his control would happen. These activities were more a form of self-punishment, evidence of his unworthiness. The demeaning activities succeeded in making him feel worse, more withdrawn and more disgusted with his life and person.

Most of his counterproductive behavior resulted from his unwitting comparisons of himself to how he imagined others felt—the others who seemed happy and well adjusted. In others words, Gerry was *comparing his insides with other people's outsides*, an inaccurate and self-defeating exercise. He resented anyone with whom he competed. In Gerry's mind, they were his tormentors and subliminally he blamed them for his state of fear and the resulting inaction.

Over time and very slowly, Gerry began to see he had constructed the cage that kept him from experiencing the freedom he craved. He began to refocus on the damage he had caused himself by blaming others for his feelings of inadequacy. In an act of humility, Gerry accepted his brokenness as an act of unknowingly transferring his pain onto others. This new reality compelled Gerry to redefine himself as a person with immense gifts of empathy and compassion. He asked for help from his mentors and summoned the courage to face his inner demons; he asked for an adult relationship with the members of his family. With this act and many other acts of living in reality, Gerry began to experience a new sense of inner peace.

EXERCISES FOR STAGE 7:

In these exercises, you are asked to recount your experience with and understandings of humility.

- Describe the times you took credit for something that was not yours to claim.

- How often do such circumstances occur?

- Do you become defensive or argumentative if you feel someone disagrees with you? Describe such situations.

- How did you act towards others when they irritated you?

- How did others act toward you when your behavior irritated them?

- How often is this repeated?

- Do you feel superior or inferior to others and, if so, why?

- Do you confuse humility with self-criticism? What is the difference between these two and where does each apply in real life?

- Have you ever experienced humility? If so describe the situation(s). Make a distinction between humility and humiliation.

- If you have not experienced humility or are not sure of exactly what humility means, what do you think humility looks like in the types of situations discussed above?

- How do think others would have reacted to you had you been humbler in such situations?

- If you do not now experience humility, how might you acquire it?

- Describe how you might recognize when to apply humility before a situation becomes heated or causes alienation.

- Where do you think humility comes from?

- Review this material with your coach to explore a workable understanding and application of humility.

RECOGNIZING THE IMPACT OF BEHAVIOR ON OTHERS
STAGE 8
ONE-WORD DESCRIPTION: **EMPATHY**

WHAT IS THE FIRST INKLING THAT CHANGE IS TAKING PLACE?

This is a critical point in a person's process. Stage 6 deals with coming to terms with the effects that our behaviors have had on ourselves. Stage 7 recognizes that humility is a key element of *"breaking out of the bondage of self."* In Stage 8, we focus on how our behavior has affected others. For example, the impatience we express when trying to direct things a certain way, the intolerance we feel towards those who don't follow a prescribed agenda, or when we use others to meet our own ends or gratification. These acts of self-centeredness result in increasing inward justification and, at the same time, outward alienation from those with whom we associate.

For those who are self-absorbed, it is difficult to see their behaviors from another's point of view. When we are convinced of our rightness, our unique ability to see all things accurately or our *"gift"* to solve the problems of other people, we falsely interpret the results of our actions as "proof" of our rightness. Other people have attempted to explain and/or demonstrate that they are capable and desirous of their autonomy. This type of independence is met with our condescension, even contempt. As we increasingly try to force our will, the more others pull away and the more the alienation grows into separateness rather than connectedness.

It is difficult to contemplate the full extent of the cumulative effect of our behaviors. In fact, without the humility we developed during Stage 7, it is difficult to acknowledge the impact of our actions. We might think back to the time when we yelled at the customer service representative because he wouldn't do what we demanded, or to the condescension we displayed to someone who disagreed, or even to the rude gestures we made to the person who cut us off in traffic. These are a few of the many simple day-to-day inconsiderate acts that define a combative way of life. No wonder we are full of anger or disappointment. No wonder we develop a "me against the world" attitude. No wonder a negative attitude permeates our existence. Without facing the impact that our unconscious acts of self-will have on others, we will not receive the benefits.

Empathy is the emotional connection between your actions and the internal reactions of those who experience your behavior. Empathy involves knowing that you repeatedly perpetrated emotional blows on others and justified your acts as necessary or trivial. These impacts are significant, although that might not have been your intention. However, they are still part of your definition, the one that others see and react to, the one that pushes the perpetrator away in self-preservation.

This introspection enables you to feel what others feel. We learn to hear what others say and don't say, to read the reactive body language and to understand the subtle messages that result when others reject our self-proclaimed superiority. To overcome our immature interactions and the resulting separation, we must be willing to reach out to others with a gracious and inclusive countenance.

Empathy also involves our willingness and capacity to see and listen with new eyes and ears. Our inability to recognize the need for change stems from our being impervious to the continuous stream of information we receive from others regarding our behavior. We usually view this type of information as unwarranted and exaggerated criticism. Consequently, we dismiss it. Our frustration grows when we realize that the same messages are repeated, making the situation even worse.

Consider the following statement to better understand this principle: *"Life provides us lessons to learn with an infinite number of do-overs,"* as suggested by Bill Murray in the movie *Groundhog Day,* in which the same day was replayed over and over with minor improvements appearing in each iteration.

Empathy is also the antidote to self-will. Once empathy becomes a normalized state of being, you possess a sense of life that is no longer limited to purely intellectual interpretation. When empathy happens, you share joy with others. Gratitude becomes a wellspring of emotion that replaces a traditional thank you. Generosity replaces providing necessities. Lifting spirits replaces offering compliments. Imparting genuine self-worth to others becomes much more than just giving praise. These are the emotions of connectedness; they are instrumental in transformative change. When you are able see yourself in

this new context, you experience a great gift: the dawn of a
new life.

A STORY
COMING TO TERMS WITH PUSHING OTH-ERS AWAY

THE COSTS RICHARD PAID FROM A LACK OF TRUST

Richard couldn't have been any less aware of the costs he paid for not listening to the older, wiser and truly caring people who had tried to guide him in his early life and career. His attitude was rooted in a sense of entitlement that stemmed from a fanciful belief that he was destined for greatness, and it would happen without hard work or preparation. Rick appeared incapable of having a firm grasp of reality—a workable plan and clear attainable goals. When it came to girls it was not enough that a girl liked him; he needed them to adore him. Grandiosity became his preferred way of life because, in the illusion of success, failure didn't exist. If Richard could redefine objectives when an endeavor failed or blame others for getting in his way, he could continue to stumble from one scheme to another.

Rick was an imaginative, artistic child, full of exuberant energy; he crossed every boundary imposed on him. His father was an unsuccessful traveling salesman who was both physically and emotionally unavailable. His mother had a Victorian upbringing and was a strict, between-the-lines disciplinarian. The family had little money for anything other than the basics and had little tolerance for fun or creativity. Rick withdrew into his imagination early in his life, and learned to keep his daydreams to himself because he knew they wouldn't be understood or appreciated.

Because of a learning disability, Rick was a poor student, which only added to his sense of alienation. He understood he would need to accomplish his dreams on his own without any support. This process began a self-defeating, delusional cycle in which he conquered an idea, worked out details in his head, and succeeded, all without actually doing anything. Richard never told anyone because he was certain they would ridicule him.

With little money or idea of how to raise capital, Rick started his own business. This was early in his professional years; he had started a family. The new financial decision placed stressed on his wife and their finances and eventually resulted in a divorce and bankruptcy, not to mention emotional devastation. These catastrophic events set the stage for Rick to face his true reality, perhaps for the first time in his life. He couldn't escape failure or blame others any longer. It became obvious that his lack of trust in the people who could have advised him only brought him harm, not to mention a series of poor decisions. The consequences of his lack of trust in those who could have advised him, and his poor decision-making, had negatively impacted him and all who loved him.

The lessons Rick refused to learn, or even acknowledge, continued to present themselves. The ancient saying, *When the student is ready the teacher will appear,* became Rick's reality. This full set of events opened him, enabling him to listen and absorb the wisdom all around him. Rick became more willing to trust that he would receive what he needed from the shared wisdom of those who had learned from failure. He overcame his fear of humiliation and the need to protect his ego. This transformation came with a new and blissful sense of being present. Rick felt a genuine connection to his time and place.

The path to accepting his own behavior wasn't short or easy. Everything he thought and felt was based on his fear of not being accepted: his revelation of how his early years had driven him into isolation, the habits he developed to hold himself apart and withhold love from those who loved him, the need to provide for himself through fantasy and imagined accolades. Rick slowly came to terms with his lack of self-trust, as well as his inability to trust others.

It was difficult for him to face the impact these patterns had on so many aspects of his life. Honesty wouldn't have been possible had it not been for those precious few men who listened without judgment, supported him and shared their similar stories. In this process, Rick became cognizant of all the people in his previous life who had tried to help, but whom he greeted with scorn. Rick got to a place where he knew he could do things differently and where he knew he could give back to others who needed his support and guidance.

EXERCISES FOR STAGE 8:

Empathy is more than an idea; it is the recognition of the feelings others are experiencing.

- Make a list of your acquaintances (either current or past, co-workers, schoolmates, girlfriends, authority figures, or other casual acquaintances) with whom your inappropriate attitudes were on full display. What do you imagine they might have felt about your attitudes?

- Discuss times when you held yourself apart from a group. Explain your motivations in these situations.

- Discuss times when you imposed yourself in a group to which you hadn't been invited. Explain your motivations.

- Write a brief description of how you acted in these situations.

- This description of your behavior may include the following:

- attempting to dominate

- acting in a needy fashion

- being obtuse when asking for what you wanted

- In these situations, what was the impact of your behaviors, based on the way others reacted?

- How do you feel about your role in difficult relationships? Does your role make the situation better or worse?

- Have you thought of going back to these individuals and taking responsibility for your behavior? How would you go about such interaction?

- Are there specific individuals with whom you need to make specific apologies or restitution? Who are they and why?

- Review all your responses with your coach.

TAKING RESPONSIBILITY AND DEFINING NEW BEHAVIORS
STAGE 9
ONE-WORD DESCRIPTION: **JUSTICE**

WHEN DO WE HURT THE PEOPLE MOST IMPORTANT IN OUR LIVES?

With the experience in Stage 5 you revealed behavior patterns with some trusted acquaintances. Now, with the additional work of Stages 6, 7 and 8, you are ready to go deeper with individuals who are more important in your life.

For this stage, you should consider a special group of people. You have a long-standing and emotional bond with this group of people and your behavior has profoundly impacted them. Some common examples include wives or ex-wives where children are involved, the children themselves, parents, siblings, and other close relationships. These people are defenseless and they are deeply affected by your self-centered behavior. Similarly, these are the people you want most to control because their approval matters to you.

The people close to you need you to recognize and take responsibility for your past behavior. However, a simple acknowledgement isn't sufficient. You must go to the next level and define what behaviors they can expect from you in the future. This act of contrition, combined with your commitment for new behavior, is similar to Stage 3—your commitment to specific change. This agreement you have with your loved ones is more than a simple "I'm sorry." It provides hope that they can expect real change in the relationship.

It makes no difference whether the people in your life are negative, manipulative and/or domineering. You are taking responsibility and defining new behaviors to reset your own orientation. Their willingness to examine their part in a relationship isn't an issue. They might choose to take responsibility for their own behavior or they might not. Your individual act of change gives others the right to be themselves, without any expectations.

Without well-crafted dialogue, parents, for example, may take on guilt by attaching your disclosure to their own poor choices. Even though this may be true, the purpose is to focus on your reality, not to subtly transfer blame to anyone else. Other people may be at a place in their lives where this type of discussion would dredge up painful memories, and doing so can cause damage if someone limits the discussion to only the problems of the past. Therefore, this process should emphasize the improvements that others can expect. *This* promotes a positive message.

You don't need to ask for forgiveness from the people you're addressing. Taking responsibility and defining new behaviors is sufficient. In effect, you are forgiving yourself, which is more powerful than what anyone else can provide. This acknowledgement is more effective than an apology, because taking responsibility for your past behavior is an act of dramatic honesty; it removes the barriers you previously felt in the relationship. When people cross this threshold, they experience freedom in a way they never knew possible.

The following statement encompasses the message of this step: "*One's negative character traits make them human but their honesty about these character traits makes them lovable.*" When we accept our imperfections but still feel lovable, we are able to approach relationships with a heartfelt embrace.

As you approach your loved ones, eager to broach a new beginning, the past vanishes, even though the other party may still hold resentments. All the personal affronts you felt compelled to confront disappear from your motives and actions. In this act, you are setting yourself free from old patterns and unresolved issues. It's not that the other person will change because of your actions; rather the change is your taking responsibility for your actions. Consequently, you accept yourself for who you are and you offer them the same acceptance. The new reality is the understanding that both parties have faults, challenges, blind spots and distractions, and yet, both are worthy of giving and receiving love even though they might not be capable of it.

Humility and empathy have made it possible for you to rise above the past and possess new characteristics of acceptance, forgiveness, and humility. Here change has begun; new awareness and attitudes bring about new behavior, and a new reality is put into place.

A STORY
PLANNING A NEW REALITY

NEIL'S FINDING THE ABILITY TO LOVE UNCONDITIONALLY AND BE LOVED

Neil knew only one way to relate to others: he needed them to need him. This codependency was all consuming, but left him fearful that his wife would eventually leave him. This belief led to his pathetic groveling for attention and affection. Unfortunately, Neil had married a beautiful woman who was also codependent. She flaunted herself in front of other men, which kept Neil trapped in his anxiety, terrified his fears were coming true.

As Neil looked back over his life, he spoke gingerly about his family of origin. His older brother was favored because of his athletic ability and his younger sisters didn't pay much attention to him. Lost in the frenetic activity of a large family, Neil didn't assert himself, nor did he seek either positive or negative attention. Neil remembers there being incest, when his siblings and female cousins got together. Neil was not the focus of the girls' attention, but stood on the sidelines wanting what his brother was receiving. Neil left as a voyeur with painful loneliness.

His first marriage was to a woman who showed little emotional energy. Although they had two children, Neil was an observer rather than a participant. Professionally Neil excelled as an independent contractor working for private clients. He was skilled and could complete work quickly, spending long hours alone in his shop. A girl who worked in the business office nearby was equally bored and looking for some distraction. Both Neil and the girl were married with families, but began an affair that lasted for over a year. Both sought divorces to be free to marry each other.

It didn't take long for their codependent tendencies to surface. His new wife was certain that Neil was having another affair and forbade him from working at the same location. He complied out of fear. Yet, on a business trip for her company, she had a one-night stand. Neil couldn't confront her behavior, let alone rationalize it. His swirling emotions of shame, guilt, anger, and panic paralyzed him and kept him from confronting the situation.

Neil began his process knowing that he was flawed; he was willing to look squarely at himself as an integral part of his dysfunctional existence. However, he couldn't shake the need for his wife to own up to her issues. When they went to their therapist, Neil complained that the focus was only on him and that she wasn't held accountable for her behavior. This infuriated Neil to the point he threatened all manner of reprisal. He couldn't control her attitudes or manner, and all his efforts (which continued for the next two to three years), didn't accomplish anything except to make him angrier and feeling more depressed.

Slowly Neil began to take care of himself rather than wanting his wife to take care of him. He learned to set boundaries that defined his behavior instead of hers. He schooled himself, learning to accept that her behavior was a reflection of her rather than a definition of him. In time, his resentment faded and he started to believe that he would be just fine if she left him. Neil possessed a new inner strength. He let go of the need to have her beauty enhance his image, and redefined his dependence—her image was a weight suffocating him.

Nothing about these changes was easy. Neil had to hear suggestions from his support group several times before he could make lasting change. Eventually Neil surged forward and took the lead. Once Neil became aware of the treatment he deserved, he was able to let his loved ones know how he would treat them regardless of how they treated him. He knew that they could only offer him what they had to give.

EXERCISES FOR STAGE 9:

This may be the most important set of exercises of them all.

- Make a list of the relationships that are most important in your life, such as wives, children, parents, siblings, lovers—any relationship where you feel you have treated them badly.

- Write a narrative of what might be said to each of these.

- Using the full process (Stages 4 – 8), relate what you have become aware of in terms of how your behaviors have affected them.

- Be specific with examples as to time and place, with emphasis on your actual behavior, not your intentions.

- Outline what they can expect from you in the future that will be different and will define an improved relationship. These are behaviors you will employ regardless of how someone else may act.

- Review this narrative with your coach to refine a positive message of hope so it can be used to have face-to-face conversations with loved ones.

- Make arrangements and follow through with communicating with each loved one to make your disclosure.

- Review each such interaction with your coach to debrief the content and result of each encounter.

PHASE III: IMPLEMENTATION

Throughout this process, change has been taking place slowly, but in many amazing ways. It might be arbitrary to suggest that there is a distinction between exploring change and living the change. But a difference exists when you complete the first iteration of a process, followed by when you implement the changes into your daily life.

Stage 10 forms the bridge between the improved self-understanding and your daily life. You will keep the inventory from Stage 4 in the "*top of your mind*" so that as issues crop up, you can quickly acknowledge them, treating them as inadvertent missteps rather than representations of continuing and ineffective behavior. Your work thus far in applying a new awareness is no guarantee that you have completely outgrown your tendencies. There hasn't yet been any magical conversion, but rather the creation of new awareness. Vigilance regarding your behavior is a lifelong pursuit.

In this sense, you can determine whether attitudinal change has occurred by looking at whether you can sustain the new approach over time, through challenges and interactions with different personalities. We should expect that change is neither static nor constant because every situation has its unique challenges. The way people will react depends upon individual characteristics. We seek incremental improvement, expect some setbacks, but remain on the path of perpetual improvement.

In Stage 11, we aim to live a balanced life where we practice introspection and sensitivity. If you turn away from the things that drove you in the past, what is the alternative? How are you going to define yourself? Will this leave you feeling rudderless, without a direction or a destination? On the contrary. Your internal work has evolved into a different type of purpose, one that exists alongside your career, personal, financial, and family responsibilities. You seek to balance your responsibilities with inner peace and openness.

Stage 12 ultimately addresses living life in a time and space above life's discord. You perceive all things as being managed without your intervention. You have adopted a new reality that you would have previously dismissed as ridiculous, which is, "*If you do what is right for yourself, it is the right action for everyone involved in the situation.*" This is the manner of living that involves internal honesty. While you practice empathy, you remain true to yourself. You act on opportunities that express your sincere interest in and support of others. An attitude of giving to others becomes ingrained at your core. However, what you are giving is intangible. These gifts might include giving others their dignity, being nonjudgmental and demonstrating constant concern and affection, while expecting nothing in return.

STAYING IN REALITY AND MONITORING BEHAVIOR
STAGE 10
ONE-WORD DESCRIPTION: **PERSEVERANCE**

IS IT POSSIBLE TO LIVE IN A PLACE OF PERSONAL INTEGRITY?

As you become aware of your behavioral tendencies, you become vigilant to all missteps. It is impossible for any person to be perfect in making all the right choices or saying the right thing in the right way in all situations. We are always subject to frustration, being caught off guard. *In moments of high stress, most tend to revert to old learned behavior.* However, awareness means that we now recognize when old behaviors surface, and we are prepared to take responsibility for any inappropriate way we have acted.

In the past, you may have blamed someone or something else for causing a problem. The new approach keeps us focused on ourselves. Although others may have played a part in a situation that caused us frustration, we must remember that they too are human like us. They too are subject to the stress of the moment and they have the same opportunity to face their own vulnerability. If we remain focused on ourselves, we allow our important growth to take place.

Pathologically *"dysfunctional"* family systems may be at the heart of your struggle for inner peace. Family members act out roles they have played over a lifetime and cast others in their historic, familial roles. These habitual patterns make the establishment of a new dynamic exceedingly difficult. Modern psychology has a branch that focuses on these types of families as illustrated by John Bradshaw[11] in the PBS series on family systems. In Bradshaw's thesis, he asserts that, for the system to improve, each member must work solely on himself. The process discussed here follows that approach as it is designed for the individual, the one who can shift self-perception and ultimately experience the freedom to experience self-love and self-care.

Humility plays a central role in this process. By keeping the focus on ourselves and accepting our own humanity, we can accept similar limitations in others. We can only understand or feel a reflection of what someone else is experiencing and exhibiting based on our own experience. This reflection puts what we see within the context of our own shortcomings. If we are aware of our immature reactions to situations, it's possible to have compassion for others, thereby achieving greater connection. We can strive for this genuine connection despite other people's needs.

Verbalizing our missteps, without justification, to those on the receiving end is a way to create closure to a single moment that has the potential to fester and cause damage. We must risk being criticized and we must be willing to listen to the pain

---

11   John Elliot Bradshaw (June 29, 1933 – May 8, 2016) was an American author, Licensed Professional Counselor, and motivational speaker who hosted a number of PBS television programs on topics such as Substance Dependence Recovery, Codependency and Spirituality.

others share, even if the pain is based on misperceptions. This is an exercise in our humility and empathy, a representation of our openness and a demonstration of our commitment. In other words, all aspects of the process are brought to bear on this simple act of honesty, without which there would be unresolved consternation and residual pain.

Remember, in Stage 9, we defined a new form of interaction with others. Stage 10 is where we put into practice our intention to act differently. Without constant monitoring, we might revert back to ignoring our unhealthy behavior and negatively impact those around us. It is essential to persevere, because old patterns of behavior dissipate slowly and old impulses remain strong during transitional periods. In addition, others might anticipate our old responses. Bringing a new spirit into the well-established patterns of our interactions isn't easy and requires moving forward with halting steps.

Stages 3 and 7 represent the commitment you made to interrupt old patterns. Stage 10 is an essential requirement to act on that commitment. All Stages, but particularly these three Stages 3, 7 and 10, imply constancy, the never-ending application of these principles without which true change is only an idea, not a practice.

A STORY
IT CAN'T BE DONE ALONE

WILLIAM'S NEW FATHER

William's demeanor is that of a lost puppy; he wants someone to love him and take him home. On one hand, Bill has a pure heart: he is willing to do anything to be helpful, eager to please, has a soft voice, a genuine interest in others and an open heart for children. However, Bill struggles to be assertive, deal with conflict (even mild ones), and has a penchant to be self-effacing.

On the other hand, particularly in the presence of women to whom he is attracted, William lacks finesse. Internally he wants to possess women so they won't leave him. He tries to appear a gentleman above reproach, engaging in intellectual conversation to impress them and inviting them to the fine art museum or symphony. He has little sense of timing and bores them with his self-importance. By forty years of age, Bill had not married and hasn't ever had a steady girlfriend, although he takes perverse pride in his virginity despite his intense desire for intimacy.

Bill's nuclear family immigrated to the US when he was in his teens. In his country of origin, Bill excelled in academics at his boarding school. His intellect and serious nature made him a pet of the headmaster, and Bill relished the attention and praise he received. The headmaster lectured on the evils of materialism and espoused a puritan view of sexuality. In Bill's impressionable state, he was programmed for austerity and began to view women as having an aversion to sex. He assumed that he needed to honor women's chastity and not cause them disgust by expressing his desire.

His dad was an engineer who traveled extensively worldwide, and his mother experienced stress over the absence of her husband as they settled into a new country. This caused tension in the household. At the earliest possible moment, Bill left home to pursue higher education. He found comfort and safety in academia. He refused financial help from his parents and put himself through college, eventually earning a Ph.D. He continued to refuse any contact with his parents, even after graduation. When Bill found out his mother had passed away from cancer, he could not experience grief or regret.

Bill lived a Spartan life in a small, sparsely furnished apartment close to the campus where he was an instructor with a full load of classes. He rode a barebones bike and took public transportation, bought his clothes at the thrift store, and worked out at the YMCA, all so he could put an inordinate amount of his income into savings. This hiding from adulthood was rooted in deeply held secrets and self-loathing.

Frugality to the point of self-deprivation was Bill's way of life, a repercussion from his early programming. Bill knew but was reluctant to acknowledge his apparent neediness or the aversion others felt toward his unwillingness to live more mainstream. He attempted to research his own behavior and read incessantly to understand his plight, but no amount of book learning seemed to release him from his self-imposed cell.

In therapy, Bill had breakthroughs and developed a long-term friendship with an older man who was both gentle and patient. This man had experienced many of the same difficulties Bill faced. He became a surrogate father to Bill, and their conversations provided Bill a safe place where he could be accountable each time he repeated old patterns of behavior.

This father figure came from a fellowship of men, all of whom were on their own journey of self-discovery. This provided an incubator that Bill used to reform old precepts, beliefs, and behaviors. Bill hadn't been able to change on his own, using an academic approach. With the acceptance and support of the fellowship and a nurturing father figure, Bill began to acknowledge when his old patterns appeared and defined *new ways of acting in situations that had previously been confusing and uncomfortable.* He thrived with new self-esteem and confidence.

EXERCISES FOR STAGE 10:

The following activities are less exercises and more a set of lifelong pursuits.

- Keep a journal of situations where you acknowledged or could have acknowledged awkward expressions at times of stressful interaction.

- Detail what you felt, and whether you attempted to justify your response or interpret the result in a way that exonerated yourself.

- How did the other person react when you honestly acknowledged your part in what had transpired?

- How do you feel your transparency has affected the relationships?

- Continue journaling and note if incidences of such situations diminish to a low frequency over time.

- Review your journal with your coach on a weekly/monthly basis, paying particular attention to situations where you could have been more forthright.

A DIRECTION, NOT A DESTINATION
STAGE 11
ONE-WORD DESCRIPTION: **BALANCE**

HOW DO WE FIND TIME FOR ALL THE IMPORTANT THINGS IN LIFE?

Stage 11 is where we explore the vastness of the new possibilities we are afforded when we drop pettiness, criticism, martyrdom, sarcasm, and self-righteousness. In this stage, we receive the benefits by taking a new direction. A person doesn't grow taller, get smarter, get better looking, become stronger, or attain instant wealth. Nor does a person immediately gain special knowledge, achieve fame or glory or automatically begin to gain influence. It's commonly expected that new knowledge leads to tangible results as well as power and prestige. But if there isn't this type of goal, then what is the payoff? Why are we embarking on this process?

There is a distinction between life based on accomplishments and life based on attitude. Most people are involved in careers, have responsibilities and are assigned tasks and objectives, all of which are defined in terms of limited time frames and the required results. These types of responsibilities are part of being a contributing member of society. However, if these responsibilities are a person's only goal, life becomes shallow; completing one task only gives rise to commencing the next. There is never enough, there is never an end to the treadmill. Some experts refer to this as *the cult of busyness*.

Through inner personal work, we identify the old patterns we used in our daily life. Do we view the world as a hostile, combative place? Or do we view it as open and inviting, offering an abundance of what we need? Differences in perspective suggest differences in how we express ourselves, as well as how we organize our affairs. If we are under stress, then we have a tendency to be aggressive or withdrawn and compulsively focus only on the one thing to the exclusion of any and all other areas of our lives. However, if we have a feeling of wellbeing, we respond with gentleness. Our attitudes are evident in how we spend our time. What we prioritize or whom we give our attention to is a function of how comfortable we are in our own skin. One of the key goals in a process is to achieve balance.

Balance implies that we fully participate in all aspects of our lives. If we deny ourselves an essential part of life because we feel unworthy, or indulge ourselves in some unproductive activity to soothe our unworthiness, we will need to relearn our innate responses. Choices leading to imbalance result from misplaced priorities or pathologies that have been developed during times of high stress or from early learning patterns. We need not deny ourselves or over-compensate, but rather put an appropriate amount of emphasis on all areas of our lives. Doing so will help us to have a fully functioning life.

Attitude has been a central theme throughout this discussion. It is, after all, one of the things that we have the power to change. It is an amorphous concept where concrete goals and objectives are common in constructing a plan. Attitudinal change doesn't negate goals and objectives; it only adjusts how we pursue them. When we point ourselves in the direction with goals and objectives and focus on the day-to-day activities, we not only become less concerned with the outcome, we decrease our anxiety.

Each person defines his own value for having followed this path. Some find the rewards of a balanced life. Some bear witness to an abiding inner peace as its own priceless reward. Others attain a wisdom that navigates uncharted waters. Still others indicate that the process has helped them probe into new depths of appreciation for their faith. By any definition, involvement in this process isn't just a cognitive exercise; it is a portal that allows us to connect with the inner self.

Meditation can be helpful in improving our connection with self, with our ability to be present in the here and now, and help us develop a sense of direction without concern for the destination. If you have experienced the chanting of Benedictine or Tibetan monks (been immersed in the reverberating low rhythmic tones), you likely know what it means to be transported from cognitive awareness to inner awareness where deeply held emotions rush to the surface. For many people this is a new awareness and a novel experience. Wikipedia defines meditation as, "*a state designed to promote relaxation, build internal energy and develop compassion, love, patience, generosity, and forgiveness. A particularly ambitious form of meditation aims at effortlessly sustained single-pointed concentration meant to enable its practitioner to enjoy an inner peace while engaging in any life activity.*"

Regardless of the specific type of meditation, we benefit from the practice. We are better able to establish balance in our lives. If we spend too much time on our professional pursuits, it takes away from time with family and/or recreation. If we are consumed with financial insecurity, this takes away from the peace and serenity made possible through gratitude and acceptance. Part of what must change in our inner person is our adaptation, as noted in Ecclesiastes: *"a time for every purpose under heaven."* Like attitude, establishing balance is a choice and, once taken, has a profound effect on our internal and external worlds.

Having areas of your life in a workable proportion is pictured in the following simple equation.

$$\frac{I}{E} = P$$

Where I = Intellect
Where E = Emotion
Where P = Peace

The mathematical rules for this expression show that the greater the quantity of intellect you have in a situation (compared with the quantity of emotion), the greater the resulting inner peace. However, just because greater intellect means greater peace doesn't mean you should demonstrate too much intellect. Elements in your life need not be equal; they need to be an appropriate proportional mix. Balance helps you experience peace.

In this process, the variations are referred to as direction and have nothing to do with objective results. The more we direct our behavior in a balanced or realistic proportion, the more we appear nonjudgmental, the more others will see us as kind, generous, and supportive. When we receive positive responses from others, we draw them closer, allowing them to become part of our own positive personality.

A STORY
PURSUING A LIFE OF TRANSPARENCY AND INTEGRITY

DOUG'S PLACE OF ACCEPTANCE

If you were to look inside Doug's mind, you would find a man who thinks of himself as a brilliant scientist working on important research for our nation, dedicated, with a gift of insight into complex problems and the ability to successfully argue a point and prove the accuracy of his thinking. If you were to hear the inner voice of his colleagues, they would say Doug is a brilliant scientist who is arrogant, self-absorbed, and impervious to criticism. The good news is that Doug is now aware of how others see him, and he has spent years gaining insight and attempting to modify his behavior. His efforts have helped both his professional and personal lives.

Doug began life in a family that was pronounced in its religious conservatism. His father was a successful businessman, aloof and driven. His mother was a stay-at-home mom, rigidly conservative and unapproachable. Doug grew up hearing mixed messages that he knew were out of sync with the reality he experienced. His mother, who was cold and otherwise disengaged, would tell him that she loved him too much, which felt insincere. When Doug was sure he knew something important and shared his views with his parents, he was met with a dismissive tone, with no explanation for why they disagreed.

Doug was sure that what he knew was correct, but at the same time, came to expect that he wouldn't be listened to or even acknowledged. He attempted to connect with those he felt were supposed to listen but they paid him little attention, remaining out of reach and out of sight. Whenever Doug entered a room where his mother was sitting, she would disappear to another part of the house, without a single word. At a young age, Doug resolved not to be treated with disrespect or ignored.

During college, Doug married a girl who was a mirror image of his mother. He was madly in love with the idea of being loved, being paid attention to and being the center of someone else's attention. What he got was a person with deep-seated anxiety, obsessed with her appearance and repelled by confrontation. Doug was desperately codependent and couldn't help his own compulsions to engage in a way that allowed him to be heard and appreciated. His enmeshment only triggered her need to withdraw and resulted in his feeling of being abandoned.

When the marriage ended, Doug began unraveling his knotted past and seeing his life in a new way. The initial insights he acquired were in the context of a rigid philosophic structure reminiscent of his religious upbringing. It was a good start and provided a foundation for his self-evaluation. However, he faced narrow-minded judgment in the first fellowship of men with whom he engaged. Although he tried to be accountable, Doug was punished rather than supported. However, the benefits he received were adequate enough to keep him focused on a better way of living.

In time, he found another format for acquiring maturity, one that was less rigid or confrontational. In this environment,

Doug finally learned to accept himself with an openness and transparency he hadn't known before. Within the confines of a forgiving group, Doug explored his true nature. Self-honesty brought him personal integrity and he could see that his truth didn't need to be the absolute truth. He began to value inner peace more than being right. His purpose became self-acceptance. With the recognition of his own limitations came his acceptance of others, their ideas, their personalities, their limitations, without demanding their compliance to meet his standards.

Doug remarried and faces a new set of challenges. He approaches them with a new attitude and in a balanced way, and understands that his only hurdle to inner peace is to get over himself.

EXERCISES FOR STAGE 11:

Meditation Techniques

Meditation comes in many forms, stemming from different countries' traditions and from the various time periods in history. Yoga, mindfulness, and centering prayer all provide techniques for establishing a clear sense of self. The practice of meditation shown in this exercise was taken from Gordon Peerman's[12] book on relief from suffering.

> *"When you notice that the demands of ambition – or any other form of grasping – cause contraction in your mind or body, pause and bring attention to your breathing. This exercise in mindfulness of the Sacred Breath is a first step in being able to experience the desire of ambition without suffering from the demand that you get what you want. The Sacred Breath loosens your identification with any particular mind state and opens you to dimensions of yourself beyond the suffering of getting or not getting your desires met. This Sacred Breath practice is especially powerful when you are looking out on a vista, but you can undertake it wherever you are.*
>
> • *Take a moment to position yourself where you can see outside. Be aware of sounds ...*

---

12   Gordon Peerman, an Episcopal priest and psychotherapist and an adjunct faculty member at Vanderbilt Divinity School. The referenced book is Blessed Relief, What Christians Can Learn from Buddhists about Suffering, Chapter 4. SkyLight Paths Publishing 2008

and sensations in your hands … and the coming and going of your breathing …

- *With your eyes open, on the in-breath, draw your gaze to an object close to you. As if you were watching the tide coming into the shore, let your awareness of the in-breath draw your vision close in. On the out-breath, let your gaze move out into the distance. As the tide of the breath flows out, allow your vision to drop into the distance.*

- *As you continue to follow this tidal rhythm of the breath, let your body be an open gate through which the breath of life is moving. If it is comfortable for you, let your gaze swing in and out to the rhythm of the breath. Or, if it is more comfortable, rest your gaze in the middle distance, not focusing on any object in particular, but on empty space while feeling the flow of the Sacred Breath. In time, you may wish to close your eyes, softly noting the in and out of the breath with a mental 'In' and 'Out.' On each out-breath, let your body dissolve into space."*

EXERCISES FOR STAGE 11:

Balance

- Consider the wheel illustration[13] where the outside rim is held in a circle by the spokes radiating from the center.

- As long as the spokes are of equal length, the wheel will roll smoothly along a surface.

- In this analogy, each spoke represents an area of your life. As long as there is reasonable balance in each of these spokes, life will run smoothly.

- Make your own wheel with the spokes that represent the areas of your life that need to be in balance.

- Make a realistic estimate of the current length of each spoke, calibrating the length, using a combination of time spent, priorities placed and/or areas of crisis over any given month.

- If your life is out of balance, what can you do to achieve some order?

---

13   Source: This idea originally came from the executive training program authored by Paul J. Meyer of Leadership Management Inc. – Waco, Texas

- Remember, perfection isn't the goal. You should aim for reasonable balance and know that unforeseen circumstances will cause disruption. You simply want a guide to get back on track.

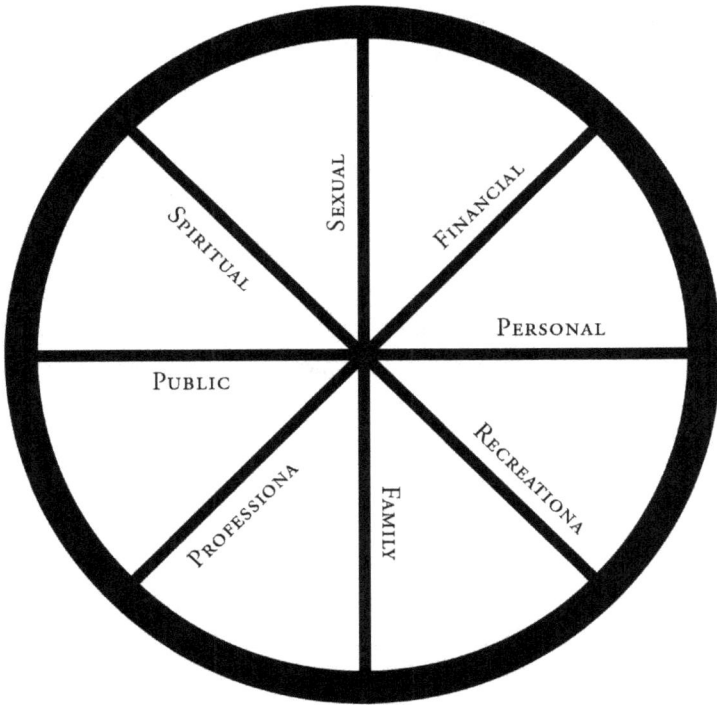

LIFE'S HIGHER PURPOSE
STAGE 12
ONE-WORD DESCRIPTION: **SERVICE**

WHAT IS YOUR LIFE PURPOSE?

Finally, this process brings us to a place that gives new meaning to life. This state of being is one of service, a selfless expression of being of service to others for no other purpose than to experience joy and peace.

Choosing peace is as simple as choosing to be focused on others. Giving is the new way of life that permeates all of your reality. Giving comes first; it seeks no thanks or recognition and expects nothing in return. It is quiet, gentle, holding abundance in your open hand for all to take as much as they need and want. Abundance is taken for granted in that we believe there always was and always will be enough to meet all our needs. Magnanimity is not for show or pride; it is for those who receive to be lifted and to experience their own worthiness.

It precludes giving things of material value. Material gifts are transitory and tend to be confused with not having enough or needing to achieve objective goals. Giving of ourselves is about discovering our unique gifts and cultivating them so we can share with others. The gift is not to be measured against a gift from another source because this type of gift has immeasurable value. Freely giving this gift is one of life's

114

higher purposes; it is an act that brings boundless energy to the giver regardless of how it is received.

We don't need to minister to poverty on the streets of Calcutta to feel the fulfillment that service brings. Being a loving and supportive father and husband can be a significant purpose in life when a person is *truly spending quality time with loved ones*. Thus, the key to finding our purpose is <u>directed intimate action that has extended connection</u>. It involves personal, emotional and genuine focus on others. Others who experience this unique place of human existence refer to it as a *calling*. It is done for no other purpose than to experience the fullness of our humanity, which is its own reward.

Many people substitute philanthropy for providing personal contact with heartfelt expressions of understanding and support. If you expect that the people receiving the largess will show you appreciation, make required life choices, become more responsible or adhere to acceptable guidelines, then they will see you as judgmental, transactional, or punitive. This is particularly true in dealing with your children. Even though your intention is meant to be supportive, predetermined objectives get in the way of true service.

Kindness is different from good intentions in that kindness is a direct act with no strings attached. Touching someone is making contact with his heart; it's different than being compassionate, something you can do from a distance. Ministry actively finds out what someone needs and fills that need using a person's unique gifts. Here we are reminded of

115

the *Beatitudes* and the great wealth available to the givers as they respond to those in need.

Service is an expression of extending ourselves outward, and it demands action. These actions of service define our behavior and character. We are no longer attempting to control the external world, but rather to support the outside world. Our process has come full circle—from a self-centered attempt to satisfy only our ego to a place of immense magnanimity filled with a sense of wonder and openness.

Is such a vision beyond reason or practicality? Not at all. People who have experienced this transformation attest to the power of selflessness. They have let go of being right and are more satisfied with being happy, at peace. You too have arrived at this place of contentment and will continue to reap the benefits throughout your remaining time. It is never too late.

A STORY
GRATITUDE AS A WAY OF LIFE

BYRON'S GIFT THAT KEEPS ON GIVING

Those who meet Byron are greeted by a rotund, jovial man with a Santa Claus personality and a heart to match. Generous to a fault, Byron exhibits boundless energy, which serves him well in helping others. Byron is respectful though opinionated, humble though strong of character, and accommodating though he doesn't tolerate fools. The juxtaposition of these characteristics is the melding of the old and new Byron. The Byron of today is an instant friend, forming meaningful connections with those he meets.

But he wasn't always that way. When Byron tells his history, it sounds like he is talking about a completely different guy. The young Byron was angry, resentful, quick to argue, with a vulgar mouth and in-your-face mentality. People didn't mess with Byron nor did Byron conform to many social conventions. Although his first marriage lasted several years and yielded two daughters, it was a battle all day, every day. Nothing was done right, said right, or thought about right. When the marriage ended, he lost contact with the girls and to this day has a strained relationship with them. These relationships suffer due to the consequences of unresolved issues and unhealed hurts.

His second marriage was very short. His wife was as angry as Byron, just as quick to scream obscenities and equally unwilling to back down. His inclination was to smack her upside the head, but this was one of the few impulses he resisted. Byron gave in to the compulsion of drinking and regularly found himself at the bottom of a liquor bottle, where there was momentary relief from the raging turmoil inside. Numbness was better than chaos, but life in a stupor robbed him of his former gusto.

The inevitable divorce left Byron alone with only himself to argue with, a debate he could not win. Having become completely demoralized, Byron looked at himself in the mirror, naked in his depression and with no real friends, and knew he had to change, but didn't know how. An unintended contact with a therapist got him a referral to a fellowship of men who had had similar experiences. This serendipitous meeting came at a time when Byron was at the bottom of his own cesspool. He instantly related to stories he heard. He knew that this place would keep him from drowning in his own waste, a condition made up of his own self-will and unexpressed anger, resentment, and entitlement.

Byron worked hard to let go of what had become instinctual reactions to life's vagaries and learned to live by a set of principles that had brought others their inner peace. He now wanted peace too. The living examples of these men motivated him. Byron became more dedicated to these principles and discovered a confidence that he could incorporate them in his life. The work would be a pursuit over a second lifetime, but it didn't matter. Byron came to understand the he would never end up in a perfect place. He only had the present moment. Byron knew that he could make the choice to experience peace and happiness in his life.

Byron hadn't known that it was possible to live life in the moment and be content. Living this way felt like a gift, one he knew he didn't deserve, nor could ever repay. It wasn't a conscious thought that led to his understanding of his new life purpose. It was more a gentle, imperceptible nudge that opened his heart and caused him to give to others for the pure pleasure of giving. Others perceived his behavior as acts of kindness, but Byron knew differently. The act of giving came from a deep place of profound gratitude for what he had received.

A life dedicated to giving meant Byron was giving to himself. His expressions of gratitude were acts of renewal and recommitment to his adopted way of living. It meant that those who received his gifts could themselves find this same gratitude and thereby pay it forward. Like the fabled spring that was the *fountain of youth* that gave eternally to those who partook, Byron had become a drop of water in the *fountain of gratitude* that provides an eternal stream of love.

EXERCISES FOR STAGE 12:

Giving is a way of life.

- What is your special gift?

- Are you uncertain of what your gift may be? What is it that brings you joy when you do it regardless of whether anyone knows what you're doing? (In this case joy is the focus, not gratification.)

- Do you feel shame that your gift is insignificant and won't be appreciated? How can you redefine what you have to offer?

- Identify where and to whom you can be of service. The closer to home the service is exercised the more meaningful and rewarding it will be.

- Are you afraid you will be wasting your time if you become a giver? How can your efforts define your own wellbeing as much as for those receiving your service?

- How would you have liked to be treated by a mentor, teacher or big brother? How can you find opportunities to provide that type of service to others?

- Do three things each day for others without them knowing that you did it. If they find out it was you who did something for them, it won't count.

- Talk to your coach to amplify on these experiences.

CONCLUDING STATEMENT

I invite you to follow this well-worn path to experience your own *sacred space*. You can have confidence that others have found a value and relief in this transformational process; others have experienced a transformation that cheerfully manages disappointment or misunderstandings; they have been set free to live lives without debilitating fear or arrogance; they have learned to practice the art of giving, particularly giving to themselves, without guile or guilt.

In its entirety, this process may seem confusing, even overwhelming. You might be discouraged before even beginning, due to the length of the process and the depth that is required. Some people might dismiss the effort because it seems there is little new or compelling. If you are actively involved in a service community, you may feel intimately connected to a goodness in yourself and others that is complete in its own content and practice.

There are a number of reasons you might choose not to follow this particular path. People who resist this path and opt for alternative venues believe wholeheartedly in their beliefs. You should rest easy knowing that you are not required to undertake this approach. No one should be judged for taking a route of his own choosing or for not undertaking an enterprise at all. Life unfolds for each of us in a unique way, based on our life circumstances and individual talents.

However, those who are less diligent, less honest or less committed may not acquire the benefits of the process.

Remember, the purpose of this undertaking is to examine your personal core beliefs, attitudes, and behaviors so you can experience a more satisfying and peaceful existence. Without challenging yourself to be completely honest and open, you are unlikely to experience lasting change. Without dedication and consistent effort to gain insight into your thoughts, attitudes and behavior, life will likely remain static, your personal growth will be stunted, your relationships will be truncated, and a malaise will take over.

The many voices that have embarked upon this journey to self-discovery testify to transformational change made possible through this process—with hard work and insight come benefits, peace, acceptance. Although daunting, others have undertaken the journey and gleaned the benefits. Current self-help literature, television personalities, motivational speakers, church teachings, eastern religions, 12-step programs for every compulsion, life coaches, websites with inspiring quotes, and so many other variations provide a similar message, each using different words and outlines.

Joseph J. Campbell,[14] a favorite spokesman, expresses the "*similarity in the diversity of beliefs.*" He was a real scholar who read the full range of ancient texts, witnessed a multitude of rituals firsthand, and interviewed a full range of religious and mystical leaders. His asserts that nearly all belief systems have

---

14 Joseph John Campbell (March 26, 1904 – October 30, 1987) was an American writer and lecturer, best known for his work in Comparative Mythology. His philosophy is often summarized by his phrase: "Follow your Bliss." Much of his thought is expressed in the PBS series The Power of Myth. (The word myth is not meant to connote "fairy tale" or something fanciful. Rather it refers to a deep-seated belief that explains life's mysteries without proof or justification.)

a similar purpose, which he defines as "*bliss,*" a "*transcendent*" state of being at peace with one's self.

While we deeply appreciate all those who have contributed to self-awareness and self-actualization, the process I describe in this book is its own approach. It mirrors the experience of the author and employs a process found to be useful when entering a place of acceptance, forgiveness, and humility. It is a process that was given to the author as a gift with no strings. In return, there are no expectations; only with gratitude the lessons included here are offered to others in the same spirit. For all who care to, I say Good Speed to you and your clients as you embark upon this journey.

APPENDIX I

Included on the following pages are a few examples of how others summarize a process to derive change. I have made no attempt to be inclusive or exhaustive in the examples provided. I have also chosen not to include a bibliography, as the enormity of information would be overwhelming.

The problem with focusing too much on the experience of others is that it detracts from your inner personal work, which is at the heart of self-discovery and growth.

However, I encourage you to read as much material as is helpful.

PROMISES:
AL-ANON LITERATURE

If we willingly surrender ourselves to the spiritual discipline of the 12 Steps, our lives will be transformed.

- *We will become mature, responsible individuals with a great capacity for joy, fulfillment and wonder.*

- *Though we may never be perfect, continued spiritual progress will reveal to us our enormous potential.*

- *We will discover that we are both worthy of love and loving. We will love others without losing ourselves, and will learn to accept love in return.*

- *Our sight, once clouded and confused, will clear and we will be able to perceive reality and recognize truth.*

- *Courage and fellowship will replace fear.*

- *We will be able to risk failure to develop new, hidden talents.*

- *Our lives, no matter how battered and degraded, will yield hope to share with others.*

- *We will begin to feel and will come to know the vastness of our emotions, but we will not be slaves to them.*

- *Our secrets will no longer bind us in shame.*

- *As we gain the ability to forgive ourselves, our families, and the world, our choices will expand.*

- *With dignity we will stand for ourselves, but not against our fellows.*

- *Serenity and peace will have meaning for us, as we allow our lives and the lives of those we love to flow day by day with God's ease, balance and grace.*

- *No longer terrified, we will discover we are free to delight in life's paradox, mystery and awe.*

- *We will laugh more.*

- *Fear will be replaced with faith, and gratitude will come naturally as we realize that our Higher Power is doing for us what we cannot do for ourselves.*

PROMISES: ALCOHOLICS ANONYMOUS, BIG BOOK

If we are painstaking about this phase of our development, we will be amazed before we are halfway through.

- *We are going to know a new freedom and a new happiness.*

- *We will not regret the past nor wish to shut the door on it.*

- *We will comprehend the word serenity and we will know peace.*

- *No matter how far down the scale we have gone, we will see how our experience can benefit others.*

- *That feeling of uselessness and self-pity will disappear.*

- *We will lose interest in selfish things and gain interest in our fellows.*

- *Self-seeking will slip away.*

- *Our whole attitude and outlook upon life will change.*

- *Fear of people and economic insecurity will leave us.*

- *We will intuitively know how to handle situations which used to baffle us.*

- *We will suddenly realize that God is doing for us what we could not do for ourselves.*

Are these extravagant promises? We think not. They are being fulfilled among us—sometimes quickly, sometimes slowly. They will always materialize if we work for them.

HOW IT WORKS
CHAPTER 5
ALCOHOLICS ANONYMOUS, BIG BOOK

Rarely have we seen a person fail who has thoroughly followed our path. Those who do not recover are people who cannot or will not completely give themselves to this simple program, usually men and women who are constitutionally incapable of being honest with themselves. There are such unfortunates. They are not at fault; they seem to have been born that way. They are naturally incapable of grasping and developing a manner of living that demands rigorous honesty. Their chances are less than average. There are those, too, who suffer from grave mental and emotional disorders, but many of them are able to recover if they have the capacity to be honest.

Our stories disclose in a general way what we used to be like, what happened, and what we are like now. If you decided you want what we have and are willing to go to any length to get it - then you are ready to take certain steps.

At some of these we balked. We thought we could find an easier, softer way. But we could not. With all the earnestness at our command we beg of you to be fearless and thorough from the very start. Some of us have tried to hold on to our old ideas and the result was nil until we let go absolutely.

Remember we deal with alcohol - cunning, baffling, and powerful. Without help it is too much for us, but there is One who has all power - that one is God. May you find God now!

f

Half measures availed us nothing. We stood at the turning point. We asked for His care and protection with complete abandon.

Here are the steps we took as a program of recovery:

1. *We admitted we were powerless over alcohol - that our lives had become unmanageable.*

2. *Came to believe a power greater than ourselves could restore us to sanity.*

3. *Made a decision to turn our will and our lives over to the care of God, as we understood Him.*

4. *Made a searching and fearless moral inventory of ourselves.*

5. *Admitted to God, to ourselves and another human being the exact nature of our wrongs.*

6. *Were entirely ready to have God remove all our defects of character.*

7. *Humbly asked him to remove our shortcomings.*

8. *Made a list of all persons we had harmed and became willing to make amends to them all.*

9. *Made direct amends to such people except to do so would injure them or others.*

10. *Continued to take personal inventory and when we were wrong promptly admitted it.*

11. *Sought through prayer and meditation to improve our conscious contact with God, as we understood Him, praying only for knowledge of his will for us and the power to carry that out.*

12. *Having had a spiritual awakening as a result of these steps we tried to carry the message to alcoholics and to practice these principles in all our affairs.*

Many of us exclaimed, "What an order! I can't go through it." Do not be discouraged, no one among us has been able to maintain anything like perfect adherence to these principles. We are not saints. The principles we have set down are guides to progress. We claim spiritual progress rather than spiritual perfection.

Our personal adventures before and after make clear three pertinent ideas:

1. *That we were alcoholic and could not manage our own lives.*

2. *That probably no human power could have relieved our alcoholism.*

3. *That God could and would if God were sought.*

Tony Robbins, *Personal Coach and Lecturer*

WHY DO YOU DO WHAT YOU DO?
THIS OUTLINE WAS TRANSCRIBED FROM A TED TALKS PRESENTATION

The most powerful internal force is EMOTION

The most powerful MOTIVATIONS are:

- *to Contribute*
- *to Connect*

MASTER LEVELS

- *Achievement – this is intellectual*
- *Fulfillment – this is an art involving Appreciation and Contribution*

What is your MINDSET

- *Biography is Future: what has happened will continue to happen*
- *Decision is Power: make a <u>lasting</u> commitment*
- *Reasons for assuming Failure*
  - *Focusing on Missing Resources*
- *Reasons for achieving Success*
  - *Having Resourcefulness, Emotional Fitness*
  - *Having Creativity*

- *Being Playful, Having Fun*

DECISION is DESTINY

- *Awareness, Emotionally Focusing on what you Want*
  - *Focus gives Meaning*
  - *Meaning directs Action*
- *Your Dominant Emotion, Your Psychological Strength*
- *Awareness of your Filter*

STATE (*of mind*)

- *What is your Model of the world?*
  - *TARGET: what are you after?*
  - *DIRECTION: what is your map (belief system)?*
  - *FUEL*

SIX NEEDS of Fulfillment

<u>Personality Needs</u>
- *Certainty*
- *Uncertainty - Variety*
- *Significance*
- *Connection*

<u>Spiritual Needs - Fulfillment</u>
- *Growth*
- *Giving - Calling*

DESIDERATA
THAT WHICH IS TO BE DESIRED

Go Placidly *amid the noise and the haste and remember what peace there may be in silence.*

As *far as possible, without surrender, be on good terms with all persons. Speak your truth quietly and clearly, and listen to others, even the dull and the ignorant-- they too have their story. Avoid loud and aggressive persons; they are vexatious to the spirit.*

If *you compare yourself to others, you may become bitter or vain, for there will always be greater and lesser people than yourself. Enjoy your achievements as well as your plans. Keep interested in your own career, however humble; it is a real possession in the changing fortunes of time. Exercise caution in your business affairs for the world is full of trickery. But let this not blind you to what virtue there is, many people strive for high ideals, and everywhere life is full of heroism.*

Be *yourself. Especially do not feign affection. Don't be cynical about love, for in the face of all aridity and disenchantment, love is as perennial as the grass.*

Take *kindly the counsel of the years, gracefully surrendering the things of youth. Nurture strength of spirit to shield you in sudden misfortune. But do not distress yourself with dark imaginings. Many fears are born of fatigue and loneliness.*

Beyond *wholesome discipline, be gentle with yourself. You are a child of the universe no less than the trees and the stars; you have a right to be here. And whether or not it is clear, no doubt the universe is unfolding as it should. Therefore, be at peace with your Higher Power, whatever you conceive it to be.*

And *whatever your labors and aspirations, in the noisy confusion of life, keep peace in your soul. With all its sham, drudgery and broken dreams, it is still a beautiful world.*

Be *cheerful.*

Strive *to be happy.*

"**Desiderata**" *(Latin: "desired things")* is a 1927 poem by Max Ehrmann (September 26, 1872 – September 9, 1945) who was an American writer, poet, and attorney from Terre Haute, Indiana.

THE BEATITUDES

THE BIBLE (NEW INTERNATIONAL), BOOK OF MATTHEW, FROM THE SERMON ON THE MOUNT

- *Blessed are the poor in spirit: for theirs is the kingdom of Heaven.*
- *Blessed are those who mourn: for they will be comforted.*
- *Blessed are the meek: for they will inherit the earth.*
- *Blessed are those who hunger and thirst for righteousness: for they will be filled.*
- *Blessed are the workers of mercy: for they will be shown mercy.*
- *Blessed are the pure in heart: for they will see God.*
- *Blessed are the peacemakers: for they will be called children of God.*
- *Blessed are those who are persecuted for righteousness sake: for theirs is the kingdom of heaven.*

WHAT IS LIFE TRYING TO TEACH YOU TODAY
ADAPTED FROM THEQUEENCODE.COM

- *Anyone who annoys you is teaching you patience.*
- *Anyone who abandons you is teaching you self-reliance.*
- *Anyone who angers you is teaching you forgiveness.*
- *Anyone who blames you is teaching you discernment.*
- *Anyone who assumes to control you is teaching you compassion.*
- *Anything you hate is teaching you unconditional love.*
- *Anything you fear is teaching you courage.*
- *Anything you can't control is teaching you humility.*

APPENDIX II

THE STORY OF JUMPING MOUSE
A NATIVE AMERICAN LEGEND – NATION UNKNOWN

Once there was a mouse. He was a busy mouse, searching everywhere, touching his whiskers to the grass and looking. He was busy as all mice are, busy with mice things. But once in a while he would hear an odd sound. He would lift his head, squinting hard to see, his whiskers wiggling in the air and he would wonder. One day he scurried up to a fellow mouse and asked him, "Do you hear a roaring in your ears, my brother?"

"No, no," answered the other mouse, not lifting his busy nose from the ground. "I hear nothing. I am busy now. Talk to me later."

He asked another mouse the same question and the mouse looked at him strangely. "Are you foolish in your head? What sound?" he asked, and slipped into a hole in a fallen cottonwood tree.

The little mouse shrugged his whiskers and busied himself again, determined to forget the whole matter. But there was the roaring again. It was faint, very faint, but it was there. One day, he decided to investigate the sound just a little. Leaving the other busy mice, he scurried a little way and listened again. There it was. He was listening hard when suddenly, someone said hello.

"Hello, little brother," the voice said, and the mouse almost jumped right out of his skin. He arched his back and tail and was about to run.

"Hello," again said the voice. "It is I, Brother Raccoon." And sure enough it was.

"What are you doing here all by yourself, little brother?" asked the raccoon. The mouse blushed and put his nose almost into the ground.

"I hear a roaring in my ears and I am investigating it," he answered timidly.

"A roaring in your ears?" replied the raccoon as he sat down with him. "What you hear, little brother, is the river."

"The river?" Mouse asked curiously. "What is a river?"

"Walk with me and I will show you the river," Raccoon said.

Little Mouse was terribly afraid, but he was determined to find out once and for all about the roaring. *I can return to my work*, he thought, *after this thing is settled, and possibly this thing may aid me in all my busy examining and collecting. And my brothers all said it was nothing. I will show them. I will ask Raccoon to return with me and I will have proof.*

"All right, Raccoon, my brother," said Mouse. "Lead on to the river. I will walk with you."

Little Mouse walked with Raccoon. His little heart was pounding in his breast. The raccoon was taking him upon strange paths and Little Mouse smelled the scent of many things that had gone by this way. Many times he became so frightened he almost turned back. Finally, they came to the river. It was huge and breathtaking, deep and clear in places, and murky in others. Little Mouse was unable to see across it because it was so great. It roared, sang, cried and thundered on its course. Little Mouse saw great and little pieces of the world carried along on its surface.

"It is powerful," said Little Mouse, fumbling for words.

"It is a great thing," answered the raccoon. "But here, let me introduce you to a friend."

In a smoother, shallower place was a lily pad, bright and green. Sitting upon it was a frog, almost as green as the pad it sat on. The frog's white belly stood out clearly.

"Hello, little brother," said the frog. "Welcome to the river."

"I must leave you now," cut in Raccoon, "but do not fear, little brother, for Frog will care for you now." And Raccoon left, looking along the riverbank for food that he might wash and eat.

Little Mouse approached the water and looked into it. He saw a frightened mouse reflected there.

"Who are you?" Little Mouse asked the reflection. "Are you not afraid of being that far out into the great river?' Little Mouse asked the frog.

"No," answered the frog. "I am not afraid. I have been given the gift from birth to live both above and within the river. When Winter Man comes and freezes this medicine, I cannot be seen. But all the while Thunderbird flies, I am here. To visit me, one must come when the world is green. I, my brother, am the keeper of the water."

"Amazing," responded Little Mouse at last, again fumbling for words.

"Would you like to have some medicine power?" Frog asked.

"Medicine power? Me?" asked Little Mouse. "Yes, yes. If it is possible."

"Then crouch as low as you can, and then jump as high as you are able. You will have your medicine," Frog said.

Little Mouse did as he was instructed. He crouched as low as he could and jumped. And when he did, his eyes saw the sacred mountains.

Little Mouse could hardly believe his eyes. But there they were. But then he fell back to earth, landing in the river.

Little Mouse became frightened and scrambled back to the bank. He was wet and frightened nearly to death.

"You have tricked me," Little Mouse screamed at the frog.

"Wait," said the frog. "You are not harmed. Do not let your fear and anger blind you. What did you see?"

"I—" Mouse stammered, "I saw the sacred mountains."

"And you have a new name," said Frog. "It is Jumping Mouse."

"Thank you. Thank you," said Jumping Mouse, thanking him again. "I want to return to my people and tell them of this thing that has happened to me."

"Go! Go then," Frog said. "Return to your people. It is easy to find them. Keep the sound of the medicine river to the back of your head. Go opposite to the sound and you will find your brother mice."

Jumping Mouse returned to the world of the mice. But he found disappointment. No one would listen to him. And because he was wet, and had no way of explaining it because there had been no rain, many of the other mice were afraid of him. They believed he had been spat from the mouth of another animal that had tried to eat him. And they all knew that if he had not been food for the one who wanted him, then he must also be poison to them.

Jumping Mouse lived again among his people, but could not forget his vision of the sacred mountains.

The memory burned in the mind and heart of Jumping Mouse, and one day he went to the edge of the place of mice and looked out onto the prairie. He looked up for eagles. The sky was full of many spots, each one an eagle. But he was determined to go to the sacred mountains. He gathered all his courage and ran just as fast as he could onto the prairie. His little heart pounded with excitement and fear.

He ran until he came to a stand of sage. He was resting and trying to catch his breath when he saw an Old Mouse. The patch of sage Old Mouse lived in was a haven for mice, seeds and many things to be busy with.

"Hello," said Old Mouse. "Welcome."

Jumping Mouse was amazed. Such a place and such a mouse. "You are truly a great mouse," Jumping Mouse said with all the respect that he could find. "This is truly a wonderful place. And the eagles cannot see you here, either," said Jumping Mouse.

"Yes," said Old Mouse, "and one can see all the beings of the prairie here: the buffalo, antelope, rabbit, and coyote. One can see them all from here and know their names."

"That is marvelous," Jumping Mouse said. "Can you also see the river and the great mountains?"

"Yes and no," Old Mouse said with conviction. "I know the great river, but I am afraid that the great mountains are only a myth. Forget your passion to see them and stay here with

ff

me. There is everything you want here, and it is a good place to be."

How can he say such a thing? thought Jumping Mouse. *The medicine of the sacred mountains is nothing one can forget.* "Thank you very much for the meal you have shared with me, Old Mouse, and also for sharing your great home," Jumping Mouse said. "But I must seek the mountains."

"You are a foolish mouse to leave; there is danger on the prairie. Just look up there," Old Mouse said, with even more conviction. "See all those spots? They are eagles, and they will catch you."

It was hard for Jumping Mouse to leave, but he gathered his determination and ran hard again.

The ground was rough. But he arched his tail and ran with all his might. He could feel the shadows of the spots upon his back as he ran. All those spots. Finally he ran into a stand of chokecherries. Jumping Mouse could hardly believe his eyes. It was cool there and very spacious. There was water, cherries, and seeds to eat, grasses to gather for nests, holes to be explored and many, many other busy things to do. And there were a great many things to gather.

He was investigating his new domain when he heard very heavy breathing. He quickly investigated the sound and discovered its source. It was a great mound of hair with black horns. It was a great buffalo. Jumping Mouse could hardly believe the greatness of the being he saw lying there before him. He was so large that Jumping Mouse could have crawled into one of his great horns. *Such a magnificent being*, thought Jumping Mouse, creeping closer.

"Hello, my brother," said the buffalo. "Thank you for visiting me."

"Hello, Great Being," said Jumping Mouse. "Why are you lying here?"

"I am sick and I am dying," the buffalo said. "And my medicine has told me that only the eye of a mouse can heal me. But little brother, there is no such thing as a mouse."

Jumping Mouse was shocked. *One of my eyes,* he thought. *One of my tiny eyes.* He scurried back into the stand of chokecherries. But the breathing came harder and slower.

He will die, thought Jumping Mouse, *if I do not give him my eye. He is too great a being to let die.*

He went back to where the buffalo lay and spoke. "I am a mouse," he said with a shaky voice. "And you, my brother, are a Great Being. I cannot let you die. I have two eyes, so you may have one of them."

The minute he said it, Jumping Mouse's eye flew out of his head and the buffalo was made whole. The buffalo jumped to his feet, shaking Jumping Mouse's whole world.

"Thank you, my little brother," said the buffalo. "I know of your quest for the sacred mountains and of your visit to the river.

You have given me life so that I may give life to the people. I will be your brother forever. Run under my belly and I will take you to the foot of the sacred mountains, and you need not fear the spots. The eagles cannot see you while you run under me. All they will see will be the back of a buffalo. I am of the prairie and I will fall on you if I try to go up the mountains."

Jumping Mouse ran under the buffalo, secure and hidden from the spots, but with only one eye it was frightening. The buffalo's hooves shook the whole world each time he took a step. Finally they came to a place and Buffalo stopped.

"This is where I must leave you, little brother," said the buffalo.

"Thank you very much," said Jumping Mouse. "But you know, it was very frightening running under you with only one eye. I was constantly in fear of your great earth-shaking hooves."

"Your fear was for nothing," said Buffalo, "for my way of walking is the sun dance way, and I always know where my hooves will fall. I now must return to the prairie, my brother. You can always find me there."

Jumping Mouse immediately began to investigate his new surroundings. There were even more things here than in the other places, busier things, and an abundance of seeds and other things mice like. In his investigation of these things, he suddenly came upon a gray wolf, who was sitting there doing absolutely nothing.

"Hello, Brother Wolf," said Jumping Mouse.

The wolf's ears came alert and his eyes shone. "Wolf, wolf. Yes, that is what I am, I am a wolf." But then his mind dimmed again and it was not long before he sat quietly again, completely without memory as to who he was. Each time Jumping Mouse reminded him who he was, he became excited with the news, but soon would forget again.

Such a great being, thought Jumping Mouse, *but he has no memory.*

Jumping Mouse went to the center of his new place and was quiet. He listened for a very long time to the beating of his heart. Then he quickly made up his mind. He scurried back to where the wolf sat and he spoke.

"Brother Wolf," Jumping Mouse said.

"Wolf, wolf..." said the wolf.

"Please, Brother Wolf," said Jumping Mouse, "Please listen to me. I know what will heal you. It is one of my eyes. And I want to give it to you. You are a greater being than I. I am only a mouse. Please take it."

When Jumping Mouse stopped speaking his eye flew out of his head and the wolf was made whole.

Tears fell down the cheeks of the wolf, but his little brother could not see them, for now he was blind.

"You are a great brother," said the wolf, "for now I have memory. But now you are blind. I am the guide into the sacred mountains. I will take you there. There is a great medicine lake there. The most beautiful lake in the world. All the world is reflected there. The people, the lodges of the people, and all the beings of the prairies and skies."

"Please take me there," Jumping Mouse said. The wolf guided him through the pines to the medicine lake. Jumping Mouse drank the water from the lake. The wolf described the beauty to him.

"I must leave you here," said Wolf. "For I must return so that I may guide others, but I will remain with you as long as you like."

"Thank you, my brother," said Jumping Mouse, "but although I am frightened to be alone, I know you must go so that you may show others the way to this place."

Jumping Mouse sat there trembling in fear. It was no use running, for he was blind, but he knew an eagle would find him here. He felt a shadow on his back and heard the sound that eagles make. He braced himself for the shock. And the eagle hit. Jumping Mouse went to sleep.

Them he woke up. The surprise of being alive was great, but now he could see. Everything was blurry, but the colors were beautiful.

"I can see. I can see!" said Jumping Mouse again and again.

A blurry shape came toward Jumping Mouse. Jumping Mouse squinted hard but the shape remained a blur.

kk

"Hello, brother," said a voice. "Do you want some medicine?"

"Some medicine for me?" asked Jumping Mouse. "Yes. Yes."

"Then crouch down as low as you can," the voice said, "and jump as high as you can."

Jumping Mouse did as he was instructed. He crouched as low as he could and jumped. The wind caught him and carried him higher.

"Do not be afraid," the voice called to him. "Hang on to the wind and trust."

Jumping Mouse did. He closed his eyes and hung on to the wind and it carried him higher and higher. Jumping Mouse opened his eyes and they were clear, and the higher he went the clearer they became. Jumping Mouse saw his old friend upon a lily pad on the beautiful medicine lake. It was the frog.

"You have a new name," called the frog. "You are Eagle."

APPENDIX III

THE STORY OF THE CRESCENT MOON BEAR

THIS JAPANESE MYTH IS FROM THE BOOK, *WOMEN WHO RUN WITH THE WOLVES*, BY CLARISSA PINKOLA ESTES

There once was a young woman who lived in a fragrant pine forest. Her husband was away fighting a war for many years. When he was released from duty, he trudged home in a most foul mood. He refused to enter the house for he had become used to sleeping on stones. He kept to himself and stayed in the forest.

His young wife was excited when she learned her husband was coming home. She cooked bowls of tasty white soybean curd and three kinds of fish, and three kinds of seaweed, and rice sprinkled with red pepper, and nice cold prawns.

Smiling shyly, she carried the food to the woods and knelt beside her war-weary husband and offered him the beautiful food. But he sprang to his feet and kicked the trays over.

"Leave me alone!" he roared, turning his back on her. He became so enraged she was frightened of him. Time after time this occurred until finally, in desperation, the young wife found her way to the cave of the healer who lived outside the village.

"My husband has been badly injured in the war," said the wife. "He rages continuously and eats nothing. He wishes to stay outside and will not live with me as before. Can you give me a potion that will make him loving and gentle once again?"

The healer assured her, "This I can do for you, but I need a special ingredient. Unfortunately, I am all out of hair from the crescent moon bear. So, you must climb the mountain, find the black bear, and bring me back a single hair from the crescent moon at its throat. Then I can give you what you need, and life will be good again."

Some women would have felt overwhelmed by this task. Some women would have thought the entire effort impossible. But not she, for she was a woman who loved.

The next morning, she went out to the mountain. And she sang out "Arigato zaisho," which is a way of greeting the mountain and saying, "Thank you for letting me climb upon your body."

She climbed into the foothills where there were boulders like big loaves of bread. She ascended up to a plateau covered with forest. The trees had long draping boughs and leaves that looked like stars.

"Arigato zaisho," she sang out. This was a way of thanking the trees for lifting their hair so she could pass underneath.

She climbed till she saw snow on the mountain peak. A storm began, and the snow blew straight into her eyes and deep into her ears. Blinded, still she climbed higher. And when the snow stopped, the woman sang out "Arigato zaisho," to thank the winds for ceasing to blind her.

She searched all day and near twilight a gigantic black bear lumbered across the snowfall. The crescent moon bear roared fiercely and entered its den. She reached into her bundle and placed the food she had brought in a bowl. She set the bowl outside the den and ran back to her shelter to hide. The bear smelled the food and came lurching from its den, roaring so loudly it shook loose little stones. The bear circled around the food from a distance, then ate the food in one gulp.

The next evening the woman did the same, but this time instead of returning to her shelter she retreated only halfway. The bear smelled the food, heaved itself out of its den, roared to shake the stars from the skies, tested the air very cautiously, but finally gobbled up the food. This continued for many nights until one dark blue night the woman felt brave enough to wait even closer to the bear's den.

She put the food in the bowl outside the den and stood right by the opening. When the bear smelled the food and lumbered out, it saw not only the usual food but also a pair of small human feet. The bear roared so loudly it made the bones in the woman's body hum.

The woman trembled, but stood her ground. The bear hauled itself onto its back legs, smacked its jaws, and roared so that the woman could see right up into the red-and-brown roof of its mouth. But she did not run away. The bear roared even more and put out its arms as though to seize her, its claws hanging like ten long knives over her scalp. The woman shook like a leaf in high wind, but stayed right where she was.

"Oh, please, dear bear," she pleaded. "Please, dear bear, I've come all this way because I need a cure for my husband."

The bear brought its front paws to earth in a spray of snow and peered into the woman's frightened face. For a moment, the woman felt she could see entire mountain ranges, valleys, rivers, and villages reflected in the bear's old, old eyes. A deep peace settled over her, and her trembling ceased.

"Please, dear bear, I've been feeding you all these past nights. Could I please have one of the hairs from the crescent moon on your throat?" The bear paused. This little woman would be easy food. Yet suddenly he was filled with pity for her. "It is true," said the crescent moon bear, "You've been good to me. You may have one of my hairs. But take it quickly, then leave here and go back to your own."

The bear raised its great snout so the white crescent on its throat showed. She quickly pulled a hair.

"Oh, thank you, crescent moon bear, thank you so much."

The woman bowed and bowed. The bear roared at the woman in words she could not understand and yet words she had somehow known all her life. She turned and fled down the mountain as fast as she could. She ran under the trees with leaves shaped like stars. And all the way through she cried,

ddd

"Arigato zaisho" to thank the trees for lifting their boughs so she could pass. She stumbled over the boulders, crying "Arigato zaisho" to thank the mountain for letting her climb upon its body.

Though her clothes were ragged, her hair askew, her face soiled, she ran down the stone stairs that led to the village, down the dirt road and right through the town into the hovel where the old healer sat tending the fire.

"Look, look! I have it, I found it, I claimed it, a hair of the crescent moon bear!" cried the young woman.

"Ah good," said the healer with a smile. He peered closely at the woman and took the pure white hair and held it out toward the light. He weighed the long hair in one old hand, measured it with one finger, and exclaimed, "Ah. Yes! This is an authentic hair from the crescent moon bear." Then suddenly he turned and threw the hair deep into the fire, where it popped and crackled and was consumed in a bright orange flame.

"No!" cried the young wife. "What have you done!?"

"Be calm. It is good. All is well," said the healer. "Remember each step you took to climb the mountain? Remember each step you took to capture the trust of the crescent moon bear? Remember what you saw, what you heard, and what you felt?"

"Yes," said the woman, "I remember very well."

eee

The old healer smiled at her gently and said, "Please now, my daughter, go home with your new understandings and proceed in the same ways with your husband."

fff

ACKNOWLEDGEMENTS

The men mentioned in this book are some of the individuals who understand that self-examination is essential for personal growth. They come from many walks of life, but all possess a strong internal compass and a desire to make a positive contribution with their lives. While each man approaches the process from a differing point of view, every one of them has the desire for deep introspection. Their lives provide inspiration to the possibility of reaching a state of inner peace from different starting points, using different worldviews, and applying different philosophies.

Each friendship has been maintained in a different way. Some are simply friends with an abiding respect for one another, a relationship based on acceptance, where we can be our true selves. Others use the friendship as a means of continually exploring the hidden source of meanings in their evolving lives. Still other friendships are simply examples of what change can offer, from lives broken by circumstance to places of gratitude.

In addition to the ones mentioned in this book, many men have contributed to formulating the ideas expressed in *A Process*. Many of the unreferenced italicized phrases in the main text come from these people. The men mentioned here represent the archetypes of those encountered along the journey. These men possess a fierce commitment to follow a structured approach to find themselves. While their characteristics are innate qualities (for the most part), the personal growth they experienced has provided an open and dedicated approach to living. Each of them is unique and separate in the way he applies the principles. Regardless of their individual paths, each man has profoundly benefited from the process. They are all inspirations.

RANDY ROHR

I recognize Randy for helping put these thoughts in written form, in order to share these ideas with others. He comes with the innate skills of communication and forming personal connections. His help in reviewing and contributing to this writing has been essential in producing a clear, understandable presentation. His dedication to the spiritual nature of personal growth has been invaluable in keeping spirituality a prime focus of this writing.

BERNIE LECLERC

Bernie is a man who brings out the "free spirit" in everyone he meets. He has a phenomenal insight into the human condition and can illustrate these truths through his gift of story telling. We have spent many warm hours collaborating on creative projects, which has added immeasurably to our friendship. His experience as a wilderness guide, his pursuit of primitive skills and affinity with Native American culture provide an invaluable example of pure humility. The phenomenal change he has achieved over the years is a testament to the benefits made possible by hard work and perseverance.

FRANK BERGNER

Over our 30-year friendship, Frank has demonstrated many of the personal characteristics that this process is meant to enhance. He is generous and freely giving of his special gift of knowledge and experience to those in need. He is supremely confident in all he sets his mind to and uses his mathematical instincts to reduce many of life's complexities to simple formulae. He has a robust sense of humor, never meets a stranger, and always sees life from a positive perspective. His pursuit of a traditional Christian form of spiritual practice strengthens his sense of inner peace.

LOWRY FOSTER

Lowry represents the quintessential seeker of truth, a passion for the overall good and questing after the best he can find. These ideals are packaged inside a sensitive, artistic actor and poet who is both loyal and quick to be helpful. Sharing some of his poems and other artwork with me has deepened our sense of connection. One of his greatest assets is his ability to accurately sense how others feel, reaching out in true empathy to support and encourage those struggling. Like the other men acknowledged, Lowry has a compass at his core that sets a true direction from which he does not deviate.

BOB NIEDER

More than most, Bob exemplifies the key changes that can be gained through this process. Coming from a place of prestige and success, his intellect serves his understanding of these principles and he helps others see their value. His path has allowed him to experience a metamorphosis, from a purely cognitive understanding to a place of emotional acceptance and humility. He expresses this change in terms of gratitude. His change bears witness to the victory available in surrender.

SANDY BEACH

The late Sandy B, well known for his motivational tapes, hosted a Saturday morning study group located in Washington D.C. which, during the 1970s, I had the privilege of attending. This is where I first started on my journey of self-discovery. Sandy outlined his unique and humorous understandings of change in pragmatic and practical terms. His approach was foundational to the process outlined in this book and remains a guiding light to all who received the gift of his life's work. His continuing popularity underscores the value that a multitude of people can receive from following a structured path.

MARK DIAMENT

Mark is among the most studious of fellow sojourners, a seeker of truth and an interpreter of dreams. He has a special affinity for working with children, due in large part to his own childhood. He gives an untold dedication to their wellbeing. His abstract watercolor art is his means of expressing the underlying spiritual ideals that come from his deep adherence to the Jewish faith. In his study of the Torah, he draws parallels between the ancient writings and the principles expressed here. This had added to my certainty that nothing is new under the sun and that transformative change is available to all who desire it and will work for it.

STEPHEN BRUNSTON

In no small measure, Stephen is the person who helped me see that a process of personal growth must be rooted in the change experiences. He often reminded me that without change, there is little purpose in pursuing self-examination. He challenged my self-perceptions, my preconceived precepts, and made me look at my persona. In many ways, my defensive reactions toward these assaults were necessary for me to break down my comfortable shield of self-assuredness. I am grateful to Stephen in that he, along with many others, cared enough to help me overcome my arrogance and pride.

EXPERIENCE AND QUALIFICATIONS

Mr. Hanson was educated with a master's degree and pursued a 30-year-career in Strategic/Management Consulting and Account Management. Some of his more well-known assignments include Wal*Mart, Prudential Real Estate, American Isuzu Motors, Bethlehem Steel, and General Electric.

Much of Mr. Hanson's own inner personal work has been done in the Al-anon 12-Step program beginning in the late 1970's. Having experienced the ravages of alcoholism on his family, Mr. Hanson has first-hand knowledge of the impact that unrelenting chaos can result in all forms of destructive behavior.

The principals Mr. Hanson has applied to his own life and the fundamental changes he experienced from the application of these principals give him absolute confidence in their power to bring about positive change.

www.ingramcontent.com/pod-product-compliance
Lightning Source LLC
Chambersburg PA
CBHW070957040426
42443CB00007B/556